Apology to the Young Addict

JAMES BROWN

COUNTERPOINT
Berkeley, California

Apology to the Young Addict

A Memoir

Apology to the Young Addict

Library of Congress Cataloging-in-Publication Data
Names: Brown, James, 1957– author.
Title: Apology to the young addict : a memoir / James Brown.
Description: First hardcover edition. | Berkeley, California : Counterpoint,
2020.
Identifiers: LCCN 2019026311 | ISBN 9781640092860 (hardcover) | ISBN
9781640092877 (ebook)
Subjects: LCSH: Brown, James, 1957– | Brown, James, 1957—Family. |
Alcoholics—United States—Biography. | Authors, American—21st
century—Biography. | Drug addicts—Rehabilitation—United States.
Classification: LCC PS3552.R68563 Z46 2020 | DDC 813/.54 [B]—dc23
LC record available at https://lccn.loc.gov/2019026311

Jacket design by Sarah Brody
Book design by Jordan Koluch

COUNTERPOINT
2560 Ninth Street, Suite 318
Berkeley, CA 94710
www.counterpointpress.com

Printed in the United States of America
Distributed by Publishers Group West

10 9 8 7 6 5 4 3 2 1

For Gary

Contents

Apology to the Young Addict

The Good Neighbors

When I think of a junkie, I see a skeleton-thin figure with abscesses up and down their arms, trembling and feverish, looking for that next fix. Or I picture the mug shot of a toothless meth-head with her face pocked with scabs. Life didn't start out this way for them, but their stories are remarkably similar, how they hit bottom, lose everything, and end up living off the streets. No, when I think of an addict, I don't for a second see a middle-class, retired elderly couple with two Subaru hatchbacks parked in the driveway of a quaint cottage in the resort town of Lake Arrowhead. When my wife and I move into the house next door, about two years before their accidents, Freddie welcomes us to the neighborhood with a batch of freshly made chocolate chip cookies. Neddy shakes my hand and tells me that if I need anything, anything, don't hesitate to ask. Over the course of the next few months we learn that they used to run their own real estate business, Freddie & Neddy's Mountain Homes, in the nearby town of Skyforest, and that Freddie, in her youth, played on our national volleyball team in the 1984 Olympics in Los Angeles.

Neddy was a point guard at USC. They're a tall couple. I'd guess Freddie to be an inch or two shy of six feet, and Neddy an inch or two over that. I'd say they're pushing eighty, and they're healthy and fit, still going strong. They even invite us to go cross-country skiing when the snows arrive later that year. It's summer when we move in, but Paula and I, we're private people, and we politely decline the offer. Besides, we don't know the first thing about skiing.

I like to remember Neddy tending to his rose bushes and tomato plants. I like to remember watching him sweeping his driveway of the pine needles and leaves that fall from the trees of the forest that surrounds his home and mine. I like to remember Freddie working alongside him, dressing up for the occasion in bright yellow culottes and a matching yellow sleeveless blouse. Her long arms are tanned and thin and she always wears a wide-brim gardening hat with a leather chin-strap dangling about her neck. They both wear matching tan suede gloves.

During the first winter in our new house, when the snows come, Neddy is right on top of it. My wife enjoys teasing me. It could be the middle of a blizzard and she'll peer out the window and spot him, all bundled up in his parka, a knit cap and wool scarf, shoveling around Freddie's Subaru while I'm sitting on the couch watching TV.

"Look at that," she says. "He's digging his wife's car out. I don't see you out there doing that for me. Whatever happened to chivalry?"

She knows I always help, but I don't see the point in shoveling until the snow stops falling. No sense in doing the same job twice. That's what I tell her. Paula just shakes her head.

Good neighbors are quiet neighbors. They don't blast music all hours of the night. Or the TV for that matter. If they have a dog, as Freddie and Neddy do, a little schnauzer they rescued from certain death at the pound, they don't let it bark and bark, especially when there's nothing to bark at. Good neighbors are friendly and say hello if they happen to pass in their yards, taking out the trash, say, or bumping into each other at the grocery store, as is often the case in small towns like ours. Good neighbors are also respectful of each other's privacy, and if they fight, as it seems all couples do every now and then, even the elderly, they at least close the windows and doors, so you don't have to hear them shout and scream. In every regard, Freddie and Neddy score perfect marks, except, maybe, for that schnauzer, which does bark at nothing whenever they let it out on their deck. To be fair, we have two friendly, gentle pit bulls, the female a mix, and she's guilty of the same when we let her out on our deck.

Then, during the second winter in our new house, Freddie slips on their icy driveway as she's getting into her Subaru. She lands hard and shatters her left hip. My wife and I are at work when it happens, so I can only imagine her lying there on the freezing asphalt in excruciating pain, calling out to Neddy. Hopefully he hears her right away. I hate to think the poor woman has to wait long for help and hope that the ambulance arrives quickly. At the hospital they do a hip replacement on her, and after a couple of weeks, when she's able to get around using a walker, they send her home. I'm sure they also prescribe something for the pain. That's protocol during the recovery period. Tranquilizers might well be in the picture, too, if the patient has difficulty sleeping. To compound their misfortunes, while she's still recuperating, Neddy wrenches his back dragging their garbage cans down to the street for the trash collectors to pick up. Now if he bends over a particular way, or turns a particular way, it sends a paralyzing jolt of pain, almost like an "electric shock," he tells me, shooting from somewhere along his spine down through one leg. His is a watch-and-wait situation, as apparently the X-rays didn't reveal much, and I'm sure that in the meantime their doctor also prescribes him something for the pain, and maybe also something for sleep, until he heals up through physical therapy or undergoes some kind of corrective surgery. The latter is a last resort, as he doesn't want them slicing and dicing anywhere near his back. He says he's heard too many horror stories about people never being able to walk again because the doctors screwed up. He says he'd rather live with the pain than spend the rest of his life in a wheelchair.

Fact is, they're in a bad way, so when Neddy calls early one cold evening, I don't hesitate to help.

"I hate to bother you," he says, "but I'm wondering if you could spare some firewood."

"Sure," I say.

"We just need enough to get us through the night. I ordered a cord last week, and now here it is, what, Wednesday, and they still haven't delivered it."

"Not a problem. We'll be right over."

"You're a lifesaver," he says. "I can't tell you how much we appreciate this."

The older cottages in the area, and theirs is one of the older ones, depend on cast-iron wood-burning stoves for heat, and you're in big trouble if you run short of wood. The only other way to keep your home warm is to turn on the gas burners and the oven of your cooking stove in the kitchen. Electric space heaters help, but not much. I lived in one of those cottages during leaner times, so I know this is an important matter, and right after I hang up I go to Logan's room. Logan is my middle son, almost sixteen. I tell him to put on his jacket, that we need to deliver some wood to the neighbors, and then I go to Nate's room. He's the youngest at ten, and though at this age he can't carry much, the idea is to make him a part of our chores, to train him, involve him.

Together we bring them enough wood to easily last a couple days. This is also when I notice that the stairs leading to their front door are rickety. Any one of the steps could give out at any time. It's a real hazard, these stairs. An accident waiting to happen. Neddy can hear us tramping through the forest to his back door and meets me on the porch. He has a twenty-dollar bill in his hand. He's dressed in baggy, striped pajamas. His thin gray hair looks like he just hurriedly combed it. It's slicked back, still damp with water.

The wood is heavy. I have it stacked in my arms up to my chin, the boys the same, but Neddy is blocking our way. I don't want him to have to carry it inside with his bad back.

"Excuse me," I say.

"Just set it there," he says, pointing to a spot next to the door.

"It's just as easy to set it inside," I say.

Neddy shakes his head.

"Freddie's not feeling so good. She's asleep on the couch. You can put it there," he says, pointing again to the same spot. "It won't kill me to drag in a few logs."

So that's what we do. I make sure the boys stack their loads of wood neatly on top of where I stack mine, and when we're done Neddy holds that twenty-dollar bill out to me.

"Here," he says.

I wave it off. I smile.

"Your money is no good here," I tell him.

"I'm sure the boys could use it."

He offers it to Logan, who knows better. Both my boys know better and it makes me proud. I may be a recovering alcoholic, and in the past, before I got clean and sober, something far from a good father, but I still like to take credit for doing a few things right.

"Be careful of these stairs," I tell him, "especially that bottom rung. It's just about rotted out."

"I know," he says. "The whole thing needs replacing. I got a bid and they want four thousand."

My father was a building contractor, and I bid quite a few jobs with him, so I can usually tell right away what's fair and what's not.

"Shouldn't be more than half that," I say, "including material."

"Can you do this kind of work?"

I think to myself, yes, I can do this kind of work, but I don't like doing it. On the other hand, I dislike people who try to take advantage of others, especially the elderly, and this is a case where I have a chance to be a good neighbor. It's also an opportunity to teach Logan something about carpentry. Nate is a little young to swing a hammer, let alone be near my father's old power saw, but he could bag scrap and old nails when we're through for the day.

Before I can answer, Freddie appears in the doorway behind him. She's wearing a sleeveless nightgown. Her eyes are glassy and her face is pale and her ordinarily tanned arms are chalky white and thinner than I remember. She looks at Logan. "Oh, how *cute* you are," she says, but she says it in a creepy sort of way. Neddy senses it, too, the tone. He glares at her. He raises his voice.

"Freddie," he says. "Go lie down. You shouldn't be walking yet."

"How old are you, young man?"

"*Freddie.*"

"Okay, okay," she says, and then she turns away, disappearing into the darkness of their cottage. It's odd, I think, because it's getting on toward night, it's hard to see now, but they still haven't turned on any lights.

That summer, when Logan is out of school and I'm off from teaching, we tear out the old staircase and build Neddy and Freddie a good sturdy one that should last them the rest of their lives. And we do it for less than half that ridiculous four thousand dollars they were quoted. It comes in at about five hundred dollars for lumber and material, and the rest is wages, most of which goes to Logan, as he's a teenager saving up for a car. What should've been

a weeklong job, however, turns into two, in part because my carpentry skills are rusty and I make a few mistakes along the way,
and in part because Freddie, despite Neddy's urgings, has a habit
of interrupting us. Sometimes it's to offer a Coke or a tall, cool
glass of her freshly made lemonade, other times it's just to talk.
She's always in that nightgown, and Neddy, for that matter, is always in those striped pajamas unless he has errands to do, grocery
shopping, say, checking the mail at the post office, or picking up
those prescriptions that I'm beginning to think might be doing
them more harm than good.

It's when he leaves that she does most of her talking. She
never actually comes out of the house. Either she talks to us
through the screen door with their schnauzer barking in the
background, or from the open window of her bedroom in their
loft, again looking at us through a screen. She seems starved for
conversation, and though I can tell she's not always in her right
mind, because she occasionally slurs her words or forgets what
she's talking about and changes the subject in midsentence, I
don't have it in me to cut her short. We learn, for instance, that
she and Neddy were high school lovers. That they have a daughter, who, Freddie proudly proclaims, is married to a "very successful podiatrist" and lives in Hawaii. She tells me what she told
me before about their real estate agency in Skyforest. Freddie &
Neddy's Mountain Homes.

"You ever hear of us?"

I say I have, though it isn't true.

"We sold it to Century 21 when we retired. That was twenty-
two years ago. Has it been that long? Yes," she says, as if to herself,
"yes, it goes so quickly, all so quickly."

She's talking from behind the window screen, so I can't see her face clearly. It's really more like a shadow, and whatever meds she's taken are kicking in. Her voice has a dreamy, faraway quality to it.

"I was a real beauty," she says.

I don't know what to say other than the obvious. "You still are."

"Oh hush," she says to me. To Logan, she says, "I would've swept you off your feet, young man. Don't think for second I wouldn't have."

He smiles but it's a crooked, awkward smile.

The day before, after we'd finished working, he looked at me and shook his head. "What's with that old lady? She crazy or something?" And I told him no, not to worry, we'll be done with the job soon enough.

"I need to lie down now," she says.

This is late afternoon, not far from quitting time, and you can't build a staircase quietly. "You want us to call it a day?"

"No," she says. "The noise doesn't bother me, and I like when you cut the wood. The smell of it. The smell of fresh-cut lumber."

Some people can have a drink now and then. They can go out at night and get a little tipsy and enjoy themselves. It's no big deal. They can take it or leave it. Then there are others, like myself, who can't have a sip of the stuff without triggering a craving for more. And more. It's never enough for alcoholics, and the same goes for these meds so many doctors pass out. The usual suspects are Vicodin and Oxycodone for pain, Ambien and Restoril for sleep, and Xanax and Valium for anxiety, and it's some that can use them without a hitch, and others, like myself, who feel that if one pill takes away my pain and gives me a buzz, two or three will make me feel even better. Tolerance, however, is another matter. That applies straight across the board for everyone. What the prescribed dose initially does for you, inside of a few weeks, you'll need to double it to get the same effect. At some point, and it doesn't take long, maybe a couple of months, the original reasons for taking the meds give way to something other than easing pain, anxiety, or sleeplessness. And refilling those prescriptions can get expensive.

I don't know what their finances are, but even with Medicare there are deductibles, and along with the regular bills we all have to pay every month, it can be hard when you're older and retired and living off a fixed income. The first things to go are the Subarus. One day I see them parked in the driveway as usual, then another day, when I happen to notice, they aren't there anymore. Neddy tells me they're in the shop getting worked on, but after a few weeks, when the cars still aren't there, I start to think that maybe they've been repossessed. Whatever the situation, it isn't long after the cars go that the calls start. Sometimes it's Freddie. Sometimes it's Neddy. I think they discuss trading off calls between themselves, so that neither one seems more of a pest, and weeks after their cars are gone, they stick to their story that they're still in the shop. It's sad, the lies we tell ourselves to save face, but I have no room to judge. I've done the same when the bottle had hold of me.

In the beginning, Paula and I try to be understanding. In the beginning, we try to be good neighbors. Paula picks up one of the first calls. We've just finished dinner and I'm at the sink rinsing off plates. She holds the phone against her ear with her shoulder while she wipes down the table with a dishrag.

"No," she says, "not at all. I have the day off. What time should I come by?"

When she hangs up, I ask her who called.

"Freddie again," she says. "She needs a ride to the doctor tomorrow."

Paula teaches at the same college I do, and she's on a three-day schedule with Tuesdays and Thursdays off. Tomorrow is a Tuesday, and though it's not exactly a free day, meaning she has stacks of papers to grade, she can still set her own hours to read them.

What Freddie doesn't tell her is that this doctor appointment is actually two appointments with two different doctors in Fontana and San Bernardino. Just the ride down the mountain is forty-five minutes each way. Combined with the visits themselves, and then having to go to two different pharmacies and wait some more to get her prescriptions filled, Paula's whole day is shot. She leaves at ten in the morning, hits traffic coming back, and doesn't get home until quarter after six. She's flustered when she comes through the door. Her face is red. She slams her keys on the breakfast counter and then tells me the story, more of a rant, really, than an account of the day.

"I thought her doctor was here on the mountain. I thought it would be a couple hours, three at the most. Now I have to stay up all night grading papers."

"Did she pay cash?"

"What?"

"Did Freddie pay the doctors and pharmacies with cash?"

"Yeah, so what?" she says, as she heads upstairs to the bedroom. "Didn't you hear a single word I said? I lost the entire goddamn day."

Paula is a straight arrow. She's never even smoked marijuana. She's one of those people I never understood, the kind that can order a drink and not finish it, or have a second, begin to feel it and then stop *because* she's feeling it. That's exactly the sort of person I belong with. I'd most likely be dead by now if I'd married someone who drank or used like I did. All this is to say that since addiction is not a part of Paula's world her mind doesn't immediately go to the ins and outs of going to any length to get what you need. At some point the doctor who starts you on the meds stops giving out refills, or won't increase the dose, so you have to get creative. And if that means seeing different doctors, you can't use Medicare or private insurance to do it because they keep records. You also can't use the same pharmacy to refill the same script from different doctors. That's why I ask about the cash.

To her credit, however, Paula does suspect that something isn't right.

"If I didn't know better," she says, "I'd swear she was high as a kite." A few moments later she comes down to the living room wearing sweatpants and a tank top. "I mean, she wouldn't stop talking. I tell you, I almost went crazy. Next time *you* answer the phone."

As the days bleed into weeks, the weeks into months, the neighbors become increasingly more reclusive. They rarely come out of their house anymore, and when they do it's as if they're apparitions, Freddie appearing at dawn on her deck in that flowing white gown, ghostlike in the early morning light. Or Neddy in the evening, wearing those striped pajamas, his slouched figure passing among the trees, the schnauzer on a leash, just before the sky grows dark. That cord of firewood he was supposed to have ordered last winter never did arrive, and when the weather turns in the fall and they're still waiting, I take it upon myself to help out. They never have to ask. I'm sure he hears me and the boys coming and going every couple of weeks, restocking his pile. It's hard to stack wood without making a racket, but he only comes out of the cottage once, and he's wearing those same pajamas.

"I just now ordered a cord. I just got off the phone. But I appreciate this," he says. "You're good neighbors. We couldn't ask for better neighbors."

He offers to pay again, and of course I refuse again, and it's the same story for the wood as it was the last time. The cord never comes, just as those Subarus never make it out of the shop. The only good part here is that he's quit talking about the cars. I say *good*, because when he lies I can see it in his face, how it makes him uncomfortable, and that makes me uncomfortable, too. So do those glassy eyes of his. When we talk, it's like he's looking off deep into the forest, but he's right there, staring straight through me.

They have friends, sure. I'm guessing they're mostly Freddie's friends, because they're all older women, but at least for a while we're not the only ones who take them grocery shopping, or Freddie to get her hair done, or Neddy to pick up the mail or to the dentist or his regular doctor here in Lake Arrowhead. I don't know how they burn their bridges with these friends, or if they just wear them out with favors, as they do with us, but for reasons unknown to me these friends eventually stop coming around. This is when helping Freddie and Neddy turns into something of a duty and a care that Paula and I simply don't have time for. We both teach. We both write on the side. We have two boys to look after—our third, the oldest, Andy, has moved out and is going to college—and they have needs, too, and we can't always just drop what we're doing and run next door every time the neighbors call. The boys are already resentful because I have them sweep their driveway every now and then to keep the pine needles and leaves from accumulating. And I don't pay them. I believe it's important that they learn to help people in need without expecting something in return.

So, when their last name of *Johansson* appears on the little screen of our phone, we don't answer it like we did in the beginning. We let it go to voicemail. The first message is polite. "Jim . . . Paula, this is Freddie. Can you please give us a call when you have a chance?" And when we don't call back, she phones again. "Hello, Jim, Paula, I know you're there. I can see your cars in the driveway. You're not fooling anyone." Then she slams the receiver down. A few minutes later she calls yet again, only this one is a plea. "Jim, Paula, I know we depend on you too much, but please," she says, in a voice that sounds on the verge of tears, "this is an emergency. Neddy's in so much pain he can't get out of bed. I don't know what to do. Should I call 911?"

Paula and I listen to the message together. I'm not heartless and neither is my wife, so the first time they pull the 911 card, I phone her back. I tell her I'm coming over, and I do. She's at the front door and lets me in.

"He's upstairs in the loft," she says. "Maybe you can talk to him. He's threatening to kill himself he's in so much pain."

I'd never been in their home before, and though it's the middle of the day, all the drapes are drawn, so it's dark except for the small light from a table lamp. The living room opens into the kitchen and there's a stack of dirty dishes and glasses in the sink. The trash bin in the corner is overflowing with paper plates stained with what looks like tomato sauce. The air is stale and musty and smells as if something is rotting in the trash bin.

I follow her upstairs and find Neddy in bed, pale as a corpse. On the nightstand beside him are five or six prescription bottles, and when I come through the door he struggles to prop himself up on his elbows. As usual he has that faraway look in his eyes.

"Anthony?" he says.

Freddie sits on the edge of the mattress and takes his hand in hers.

"No, it's Jim," she says.

"Jim?"

"Our neighbor, honey."

He blinks, and when he sees I'm not Anthony, whoever Anthony is, an air of dismissiveness crosses his face, and he lies back down on the bed. He closes his eyes and then rolls over on his side.

"You see," she says, "he *needs* his medication. It's at Rite Aid. The doctor phoned it in. We have to pick it up right now. Give me a minute to get dressed."

But she doesn't get dressed. She just puts on her housecoat and a pair of slip-ons and grabs her purse. She makes an attempt to brush her hair, but it's not much of one, and it's sticking out at odd angles. Her hip also never did heal up quite right, so she moves slowly, teetering from side to side as she walks. I'm careful getting her down the stairs and into my car, and at the Rite Aid I follow closely behind her, worried she might fall. It's a sight, I suppose. This obviously exasperated man trailing behind an old woman in her housecoat and slip-ons and wild hair to the pick-up counter at the pharmacy at the back of the store. Everyone, including the teenage clerk, has a strange look on their face. There was a time Freddie never would've left the house looking like this, but either she doesn't care now or she's oblivious, at once anxious and relieved. She gives the teenager her name and then opens her purse.

"Oh my God," she says. "I forgot my checkbook."

"It's okay. I got it," I say, as I reach for my wallet, feeling as if I'm *there*, where she is now, caught up in my own obsession again, not caring what people think or how I appear, so long as I get what I need. Hate is a strong word, and I'm reluctant to use it, especially for an old woman, who, frankly, means me no harm. Yet I'm sickened, buying drugs like this, whether it's from a well-lit pharmacy or a crack house in the ghetto. The hunger I see in her eyes is a hunger I know too well. And I hate it.

The second we're back in my car, she opens one of the bottles, shakes out a few pills, pops them into her mouth, and swallows them dry.

Helping elderly neighbors is one thing. Enabling them in their addiction is another. After this last episode, Paula and I quit answering their calls altogether, including Freddie's messages threatening to phone 911. "Let her," Paula says. "I've had it with them guilt-tripping us. I don't care what they do anymore, so long as they leave us the hell alone." The first couple of threats are just that, threats, but another time, when Neddy phones, we hear Freddie in the background scream "and tell that cunt of his . . ." Before she can finish her sentence, Neddy hangs up.

"Did she just call me a cunt?" Paula says.

I don't know what to say, so I don't say anything. I'm stunned, too.

"Play it over again."

We have it on speakerphone. I don't want to play it again, but I do.

Paula glares at me.

"I can't believe it. That ungrateful old bitch. I don't want you doing anything for them anymore," she says, "and I mean *anything.*"

Then the fights start. Often they come in the early morning hours, their shouting rousing Paula and me from a dead sleep. Freddie's voice is sharp and shrill, and because noise carries far in the forest, we can't be the only neighbors she's waking. Once we hear her scream that she's going to call the sheriff, and he screams back, "Go ahead. See who they side with." I'm guessing that these fights occur when they're under the influence, or they've run out of whatever they're on and they're withdrawing, hurting mentally and physically. Both are situations I'm all too familiar with. Regret and guilt are made worse for the drugs or lack of them. Suppressed, painful memories resurface in waves of anger and grief, and for me they most often involve my brother and sister. For my neighbors, they most often involve Anthony, whoever he is or was, and Freddie blames her husband for failing him. For failing them all. She calls Neddy every name in the book. His protestations are weak, feeble pleas to stop, please stop, but she pushes and pushes until her rage peaks, giving way to sobbing and tears, and then, finally, exhaustion and silence.

To my knowledge, no one, including Freddie, ever calls the sheriff during their loud fights, but one day we hear sirens and an ambulance pulls up outside their cottage and they take Freddie away on a stretcher. We watch from our living room window. Poor old Neddy stands on his porch, this time with a bathrobe over his pajamas, watching it all happen just as helplessly as we do. When the ambulance drives away, he looks over at me and Paula in the window, or at least he looks in our direction. His eyesight isn't good. I doubt if he actually sees us, but I still feel a pang of guilt, as if I'm somehow at fault. For what, I'm not sure. I like to believe that I've been a good neighbor.

This, if I remember right, happens in late September, and by the end of October the paramedics have paid Freddie and Neddy two more visits. I'm home to witness two, anyway. There might have been more.

I know that times have changed. I know that doctors and

hospitals are more tightfisted now about dispensing certain medications, but it used to be that you could easily get away with calling the paramedics, telling them you're in intense pain, and when they rush you to the ER you'd get what you want, or something close to it, until the doctors could figure out what's wrong with you. My own eighty-five-year-old mother was quick to call 911 when I couldn't get to her apartment soon enough, after she phoned begging me to come, saying she thought she was going to die. I picked her up from the hospital three times, and the third time I got a warning from one of the nurses. "Nuisance calls are an actual criminal offense," she told me. "Your mother could be charged, you know, and so could you if you're her POA." I didn't know what POA meant, so I looked it up later, and it's an acronym for power of attorney. I mention this only to explain how ignoring Freddie and Neddy and then their calling 911 on probably more than three occasions brought them square into the crosshairs of the County of San Bernardino.

Except for making sure they're stocked with wood, I have nothing more to do with Freddie and Neddy until December. My wife and I buy into that holiday stuff about good cheer and generosity, and by the time Christmas Eve rolls around we've softened up, at least enough for me and the boys to bring them some plates piled high with turkey, stuffing, mashed potatoes, green beans, and two Tupperware containers, one full of gravy, the other fresh cranberry sauce. There's a foot of snow on the ground and no tracks of any kind leading up or down the staircase Logan and I built. They're holed up in there and have been for some time. It strikes me as sad that they have to spend Christmas alone, and half of me wants to invite them over tomorrow, while the other half says, no, don't even think about it.

When I open the screen door, I see a bright orange eviction notice stapled to the front door. I spot the date at the top. It's already several days old. Apparently Neddy heard us coming, because he answers before I can knock. He's in his pajamas, a different pair, solid blue.

"Merry Christmas," I say.

He sees the notice and tears it down.

"Bastards," he says. "Miss one goddamn payment and this, *this.*"

From around him, I can see into the living room. Freddie is sitting in a rocking chair in her nightgown in front of the woodstove. The fire is going. The TV is on. She has a quilt covering her lap, and her face looks thinner still, gaunt even. So does Neddy's. There's a glass of wine on the end table beside her.

"You paid them, honey. I remember distinctly. You just have to get on the horn and straighten it out after the holidays are over." Then she notices the plates of food my boys and I are carrying. "Is that what I think it is? How sweet of you." She raises her glass of wine as if to toast. "Merry Christmas," she says. "Come in. Come in."

I politely decline, knowing that if I accept it'll be a long and awkward affair trying to excuse ourselves later. On Christmas morning, however, Neddy dons his parka over his pajamas and makes the trek through the snow to our place. He gives us a gift, an expensive manicure set, with two nail clippers, a file, a cuticle nipper, scissors, and a tweezer. The utensils look shiny and new, but we find the sliver of a toenail wedged into the lining of the case.

Paula vows never to touch them, but not me. Freddie and Neddy are housebound, they're broke so far as we know, and as the saying goes, it's the thought that counts. To this day, I use those clippers, and every time I do I think of old Neddy braving the cold, slogging through the slush and snow to give us that nice manicure set.

I've seen a number of people who've had to pack up and leave their homes. Usually it's two or three months after the bank slaps the notice on their door. One family I knew, back when I was growing up in San Jose, stretched it out for close to a year. Never, though, until Freddie and Neddy, have I had the misfortune of witnessing the sheriff and paramedics actually pull into the driveway of a house, get out of their vehicles, knock on the door, and take the people inside away. But that's exactly what happens, and it's a sorry sight. Paula and I watch from the glass sliders that open onto our deck.

Two paramedics, two deputies, and a woman in a pantsuit who I'm guessing is some sort of social worker, clearly don't find any pleasure in their jobs, not this part of it, anyway. You can see it on their faces, the awkward smiles, the understanding nods, the gentle way one of the paramedics holds Freddie by the arm as he helps her down the stairs, slowly, one step at time. She's in her nightgown and slippers and has Neddy's bathrobe draped over her shoulders. Why Neddy's dressed and she's not, I don't know, but he's wearing slacks and a short-sleeved checkered shirt. I figure the authorities must've called. I figure they must've given them some kind of heads-up, and that he took it seriously, and that maybe she did, too, but she didn't have it in her to put on some clothes.

It's June, nearly three years since we moved into our new house, and instead of this scene where they're escorted into the ambulance and driven away—where to yet, I have no idea—I like to remember Neddy tending to his rose bushes and tomato plants. I like to remember watching him sweeping his driveway of the pine needles and leaves that fall from the trees of the forest that surrounds his home and mine. I like to remember Freddie working alongside him, dressing up for the occasion in yellow culottes and a matching yellow sleeveless blouse. And the gardening hat she wore, the one with the wide brim and its leather chin strap dangling about her neck, I like to remember that, too, and how they welcomed us to the neighborhood with a batch of chocolate chip cookies.

The cottage sits vacant for months. Once, during a heavy rain, my wife and I hear a crack of thunder while we're watching TV, and the next morning we notice that a huge branch from one of the big oaks on their property has snapped and fallen on their house, crushing part of the roof. Another time we see a realtor pull into the driveway, go inside and look around, and then get back into her car and drive off. I expect to see a FOR SALE sign go up any day after that, but it doesn't happen, not for some time yet. The cottage just continues to sit there with part of its roof caved in, surrounded by ever deepening piles of fallen leaves and pine needles. Abandoned homes are easy targets, and I keep an eye out for burglars and vandals. We have a sheriff's log in our little local paper, and every week you'll find a report of somebody taking advantage of a situation like this and trashing or robbing the place. Everything they owned, from TVs to furniture to personal belongings, some of it probably worth good money, it's all left behind. I often wonder if they had owned a gun. That would not be a good thing for some kid or criminal to get his hands on.

Then one day, when I come home from teaching, I see a woman carrying a cardboard box down the staircase. A car is backed up close to the door. She puts the box into the open trunk and then goes back inside the house. I go over there as she's coming down the stairs with another box. I have a feeling who she is, but you never know.

"Can I help you?" I say.

She sets the box in the trunk next to a couple others she's already loaded, wipes her hand on her jeans, then holds it out to me. We shake. She's out of breath from going up and down the stairs with those boxes.

"You must be Jim," she says. "My parents talked a lot about you. I appreciate all you did for them."

"How are they?" I say.

"Dad's in a senior apartment," she says, "and Mom's in a nursing home. But they're doing good. Good as can be expected, anyway."

Her face is deeply tanned, and it has that unnatural look, when surgeons pull the skin too tight across the cheeks. Her upper lip is plumper than her bottom one.

"I'm just grabbing some of their personal stuff. The house goes up for auction next week. Come in and take a look," she says. "I'm leaving all the furniture. They have a pretty nice dining room set."

I thank her, but Paula and I already have a nice dining room set. In the box she just loaded into the trunk is a stack of framed

pictures, and on top is a photograph of a much younger Freddie
and Neddy smiling for the camera. Standing in front of them is
a little girl in a bathing suit and a teenage boy wearing a football
jersey. I pick up the picture and look at it more closely. In the
background are the smooth blue waters of Lake Arrowhead.

"Your parents look happy," I say. "How old are you here?"

"I don't know. Seven, eight."

"Who's the boy?"

"That's my brother Anthony. Listen," she says, "I'd really like
to talk but I have to get going." She takes the picture from me,
puts it back in the box, and closes the trunk. "You sure you don't
want to peek inside before I lock everything up?"

"I'm sure," I say.

I'm sure there's more to say about Anthony, too, and I'd like
to hear it, but I know better than to ask. It's not right to pry.

The house doesn't go up for auction. Instead a realtor comes by
when Paula and I are at work and puts up a FOR SALE sign with
a smaller one beneath it saying BANK OWNED. It sits on the market for months, the pine needles and leaves continuing to collect
all around it, and during the winter a strong wind catches the
front screen door and tears it open, leaving it dangling from one
hinge. When the snows thaw, I remember back to better times for
Freddie and Neddy, how they liked to sit on their deck in lounge
chairs on warm summer evenings and watch the sun set over the
mountains in the distance. I think about how I could use some
lounge chairs on my deck, so Paula and I could sit outside and
watch the sun set in the summer, and I decide to go over there

and take them. Their daughter, after all, had offered me whatever I wanted from the house, so I don't see the harm. I don't see it as stealing. Besides, if Freddie and Neddy wanted anyone to have those lounge chairs, I'm sure it would be us.

There's a small gate next to the back door that opens onto the deck that wraps around the house. I last recall seeing the lounge chairs on the west side, facing the mountains, but they're not there. At first I think that maybe thieves beat me to it, but when I walk around to where the deck is hidden by the forest, I spot them, barely, peeking out from underneath bags and bags of garbage that Neddy had been unable to drag to the curb. The coyotes and raccoons had torn into them, scattering coffee grounds across the deck, plastic milk jugs and crumpled paper towels, old corn husks and shriveled-up banana peels, the rib cage of a rotten chicken carcass, and some empty, brown prescription bottles.

I pick up one of the bottles and read the label. Vicodin. *Use as needed.* I pick up another and another. Valium. *Use as needed.* Oxycodone. *Use as needed.* Halcion. *Use as needed.* Several are prescribed by the same doctor, others by different ones. I even find an empty for fentanyl, which in another life I used to buy off the streets, crush the pills, and snort the powder. It's so powerful that it's frequently given to the terminally ill in their last days. I'm sure there are more little brown bottles in all that garbage, but I don't bother looking.

What, I think, does *use as needed* mean?

And how is it that so many so-called medications are necessary? Halcion for sleep. Valium for anxiety. Oxycodone, Vicodin, and fentanyl for pain. Combined, or used separately in large doses, these drugs are potentially lethal. What really gets me, though, is why so many doctors prescribe all these tranquilizers and narcotics when they know they're so addictive and dangerous.

I could go on, sermonizing about unscrupulous doctors and the perils of drug abuse, or gloating over how my earliest suspicions proved a harbinger of the worst to come for my good neighbors, but there's no point in it. What matters more is the call I receive a few weeks after I yank the lounge chairs out from around the bags of garbage and carry them back to my place. When it first rings, and I see that name *Johansson* on the tiny phone screen, I hesitate. I'm not sure I should pick up. Then the obvious dawns on me. They're gone. What's the harm? I answer the phone.

"Hello?"

"Jim?"

"Yeah."

"It's me. Freddie."

"How you doing?

"We're doing good," she says. "I had to go to the hospital for a while, but I'm okay now. We both are. No more, well, you know." Her words aren't slurred. I can tell immediately that she's clear-headed. "Anyway," she says, "Neddy and I are living in a seniors apartment in Palm Springs and we wanted to give you our new number. You're always welcome to visit."

"Let me grab a pen," I say.

I am glad that she called. I am glad to learn that they've been reunited. But I don't want to see them. I came into their lives when we moved next door. I met them when they were healthy and I watched them destruct, as others, including my wife and boys, have watched me destruct and bounce back. And I want to believe that in passing through their last years, as I pass through my own, that we will never again lose sight of all that is good and important and sane. I am conscious of time and I am no longer a young man.

"Okay," I say. "Shoot."

She gives me the number but I don't write it down. I don't have a pen in my hand. The line crackles, and in the background I'm heartened to hear the schnauzer bark. I'd worried about that dog and what happened to it. My brother had an old mutt with a bum hip named Goofy, and when Barry shot himself, none of us could take the dog and it wound up in the pound. I figure the worst came of it, since no one wants an old dog. I'm just glad the schnauzer didn't meet the same fate. Like Freddie and Neddy, it too had become thin and weak, skittish and withdrawn, but I picture it on the chubby side now, with gray whiskers, its belly full of treats and begging for more.

A Real Disease

'm supposed to talk. It is Red Ribbon Week on a college campus in the Inland Empire, a region of Southern California well-known for its failing infrastructure and lack of opportunities, and I'm here an hour early. I would rather err on the side of arriving with more time on my hands than not enough, because for the better part of my life I couldn't be depended on to be where I said I would be, when I said I would be, and I don't want to be that person anymore. I'm getting out of my car in the parking lot when my cell phone rings.

The connection is scratchy, intermittent with static, and I'm not sure I hear him right. I'm not sure I understand his first words, but I can see from the number on the screen that it's Nick. Nick is my sponsor, and he's helped me get sober. He's helped me stay sober, and in this story, at this point in time, I've been clean a couple months shy of three years. "Hello?" I say. "Hello?" But the line is dead. I call him back and it goes directly to voicemail. I leave a message telling him I'm down in San Bernardino and that I'll try him again when I'm closer to home. Reception from the desert valley to the mountain is poor to nonexistent.

I didn't sleep well last night, and after I lock my car I go in search of a cup of coffee, maybe an energy drink, something to pick me up. But the student union is packed and noisy, the lines long, the cashiers slow, and so I wander off campus. The donut shop on the corner is closed. Vandals or robbers smashed the plate glass door, probably the night before, and two men are covering it with plywood. Inside an Asian woman stands with her hands on her hips, watching them work. I walk on. The houses along the side streets are small and run-down. They are built too closely together. They have steel security doors and bars on the windows and one has an old couch on the porch. Farther down, on the next corner, I come to a liquor store.

As I go inside and head back to the coolers, my cell rings again. It could be just another lousy connection, but his voice sounds strained.

"Can you meet me at Bill's?"

"Sure," I say.

I'm about to tell him where I'm at, what I have to do first, but the line gets scratchy again, then dies. I text him, saying I'll meet him in three hours. He texts me back. One word.

Thanks.

I grab a can of Red Bull from the coolers, pay for it, and drink it on my way back to the college. Inside of a few minutes all the caffeine, B-12, and whatever else they put into it takes effect. I'm awake and alert when the professor sponsoring my talk greets me at the front door of the lecture hall. I thank her for inviting me. She thanks me for coming. Her students have been assigned to read a book I wrote about my experience with drugs and alcohol, and she tells me they're excited, that they have a lot of questions. I am lucky for professors like her. Otherwise this book, like my others, would've come and gone long ago. I am lucky, too, for the students she teaches. They are part of the college's drug and alcohol counseling program and most are recovering alcoholics and addicts. They are all adults, a few my age or older, and I can tell, by the weathered faces of some, that life has led us to many of the same unfortunate places. Now they are turning their lives around and want to help others do the same.

They are poorer working-class students who come from tough neighborhoods where kindness is perceived as weakness and trust is for fools. I grew up like them. I got wasted like them, and I think to myself—yes, here I am again, among my own. Here we are unlearning the things that once brought us together and replacing them with new things, new ways of coping that serve to affirm our lives rather than ruin them. If normalcy is measured by the customary, by habit, by decades of past behavior, then it is far more normal for us to drink and get high than not. All this flashes through my mind when I step up to the podium and look out across the lecture hall. Rows and rows of students look back at me. Some are slouched in their seats, seemingly bored, but most, and I'd say there are seventy or eighty of them, have their notebooks out and pens in hand.

I thank them for being here.

I thank them for their time.

I make a joke about having a captive audience. About them being forced to read my book. I don't suppose it's much of a joke, but I get a few laughs. I get a few smiles and that's enough to break the ice. Then I read from the book, not long, maybe ten minutes, fifteen tops. I've been to enough readings and lectures to know that shorter is better.

Afterward I open it up to questions. Hands rise. This is the part they usually like best, and in the process of answering I end up telling them how I used to love alcohol. The smell. The taste. How it made me feel. How, had I been able to stop after three or four or even ten drinks, I'd still be at it. At some point, though, it quit being about how it made me feel and started being about how I felt *when I didn't drink or use.* I tell them that I started smoking weed when I was nine, drinking at twelve, and by fourteen I didn't care what I put in my body. I tell them how great I thought all of it once was and how ugly it all became. I tell them about the suicides of my brother and sister and how they couldn't live without drinking, and yet, at the same time, how they couldn't continue to drink and live. I tell them all kinds of things about my experience with alcohol and drugs and how they eventually turned on me. Though I don't recall using the word *disease*, something I say triggers a question about it from a student in the back rows. She's young, maybe twenty, I guess.

"But do you honestly think it's a disease?"

"Alcoholism?" I say.

"Yeah," she says, "or drug addiction."

By the very nature of her question, I presuppose, possibly wrongly, that she isn't a recovering addict or alcoholic. So I tell her what Nick once shared at a meeting, and I remember it close to verbatim, because he had put into words what I had felt for some time: that like many other sicknesses, alcoholism is chronic, it has definite symptoms, and its progression follows a predictable course. And I tell her, in my own words, that once addiction sets in, once it develops, that if it's left untreated it'll eventually kill you just as sure as any other terminal illness.

"But it's still not like heart disease," she says. "Or cancer. Those are *real* medical issues we don't have any control over."

I didn't come to argue or impose my opinions on anyone, and so I agree. I tell her she has a good point, and that, yes, there are those in the medical community who believe that addiction isn't an actual disease. But then there are also those that do. Soon it's time to wrap it up, and because I like to leave them with a sense of hope, I tell them that although there's no cure for this thing, this illness, whatever you want to call it, you can arrest it. You can put it into a state of remission. Every day addicts and alcoholics can and do turn their lives around. We can and do regain our health, lost dignity, honor, and respect. This is my pitch, and I believe what I say.

Back in my car, I try to call Nick. Again it doesn't go through, and I send him another text message: *I'm on my way. Be there in forty-five.* I'm concerned. It isn't like Nick, wanting to meet right away, out of the blue. Almost always I'm the one asking when we can get together, and on the rare occasions where it's the other way around, it's always been with a few days' notice. He's a sales manager of a national lighting company, and when he's not traveling across the country, he does his best to spend what little free time he has with his family. Somehow he also finds time to sponsor me and two or three other guys from our group.

We usually meet at Bill's Diner, this little place with those old tuck-and-roll vinyl booths and a long Formica breakfast counter, a stone's throw from our A.A. club. Usually, if it's empty, we take the corner booth with the most privacy, and he's there when I arrive, hunched over a cup of coffee. Nick is originally from Boston, and though he's lived in California for the last twenty years, he still has traces of his Southie accent. He used to be an anesthesiologist back east, Brooklyn, I think, but he lost his license for stealing pain meds from the hospital dispensary and pilfering the same from his patients. He wound up strung out on heroin and booze, living off the streets on skid row in the old Bowery, sleeping in alcoves and alleyways until he somehow found his way into the rooms of A.A. I know his story is longer and more complicated than this, with all kinds of bumps along the road to getting clean and sober, but he doesn't like to discuss the details. Somewhere in there he burned through a marriage, as I did, and eventually landed, miraculously, back on his feet two thousand plus miles from where he started. He remarried. He began a new life.

I slide into the booth. He looks up at me. I can see it in his eyes that he's troubled, and his face looks thinner, like he's lost weight. When did I last see him? It can't have been more than a couple weeks.

"You feeling all right?" I say.

He shakes his head. He lowers his eyes, then looks back up at me.

"I went out," he says. "I got a room in Huntington Beach and stayed drunk for five days."

I have to let that settle in. He had sixteen years of sobriety.

"Just booze?" I say.

"Just booze," he says.

I don't know if that makes it not as bad, slipping after all that time, but I'm glad it wasn't with heroin. It's so easy to overdose.

I sit back in the booth. For a while it's quiet. He takes a sip of coffee, and I flag down the waitress. I ask for a cup. When she leaves, I look at Nick again.

"What do you think set it off?"

"Does there have to be a reason?"

"I guess not," I say. "But there's triggers."

"There's always triggers but never a reason. No good one anyway." He smiles, a tired smile. "You need to get another sponsor."

"Don't even go there."

"I'm serious."

"I'm serious, too. How long has it been since your last drink?"

"Three days."

"That's a good start," I say.

He holds up his hand. His fingers are trembling.

"Look at that."

"It'll pass," I say, like it's no big deal, and it isn't. The shakes, the nausea, the physical part of withdrawal is the least of our troubles. The real problem is the obsession and the craving for more when we take that first drink or drug and then try to stop and can't.

"The first week is the hardest. Isn't that what you said when I slipped, what, almost three years ago?" And in saying those words, I remember when I messed up and met with him a couple weeks later, all beat to hell from drinking and using speed. I'd had a little over six months' clean time under my belt, and I expected him to drop me as his sponsee, especially because this wasn't the first time I'd slipped. I remember asking if he wanted me to find another sponsor and how he laughed and shook his head. "People like us fuck up more often than not," he'd said. "It's actually pretty rare for drunks to get the program first time around and never drink again." So we started over. I did the Steps again. He made me commit to reading the Big Book at least twenty minutes a day. I had to attend a meeting once a day, too, for the first ninety days. I had to meditate. I had to pray at night and in the morning and anytime in between if I felt even the slightest urge to drink. "Why," he asked me, "do you think so many drunks and addicts can't stay clean? Because it's work, man. Hard work." But he also told me that it gets easier with time and if it didn't he doubts he'd be sober himself.

Now Nick has slipped and it's my job as his sponsee to act, if only briefly, as the sponsor. I tell him exactly what he told me when I slipped.

"You need a meeting," I say. "Let's both hit a meeting tonight."

The plan is to pick him up around six thirty and if he's up for it we'll grab another cup of coffee and something to eat after the meeting and talk some more. His wife gave him a ride to the diner to meet with me—sober or not he's in no condition to handle a car—so he needs a lift home, and later, on the drive back to his house, he tells me straight up. His voice is reasonable. His voice is calm.

"I have stage-four cancer," he says.

I don't know what to say. I don't know what anyone can say when someone you care deeply about tells you that they're dying. But I do not act shocked. I do not tear up. I just drive.

A semi hauling a load of logs blows past us. We're on the highway that runs along the rim of the mountain. On one side of the road are tall pines, dry and brown, stiffening into the sky, and on the other is the barren desert far below. Much of our forest has been decimated by several years of drought and you can look out over the mountains and see vast swatches of naked land where strong trees once stood, and higher up, you can make out the sagging branches and brown pine needles of more trees that have yet to be felled by the loggers contracted to cut and haul them away. But they will be back, the trees. The undergrowth. I've seen this devastation before, and when the patterns of heavy rain and snow return, the forest will replenish itself.

"When did you find out?" I say.

"A week ago."

I think of his wife. I think of their children. They have three daughters. I would think of them first if this were about me.

"How's your family taking it?" I say.

"I haven't told them," he says.

I don't say anything to that because I'm not sure what I would do or say if I knew I was dying. I've never thought about it until now, and I don't mean death. I have thought about death plenty of times, but I've never considered what it would be like to tell those who most love me, knowing that it will hurt them. That it will burden them. I think the burden would be worse because they would begin to think about what they need to do for the dying and there is nothing you can do for the dying, not really, except comfort them as best you can and then move on with your own life when they pass. I know that role well enough. I served it with my father. I served it with my mother, and I coped, poorly, with the sudden and unnecessary deaths of my two older siblings. I also know that if someone I loved didn't tell me they were dying that I would later resent them for denying me the choice of how I wanted to spend with them what little time they had left. I don't suppose, if it were me instead of Nick, that that choice would be mine to make. I don't suppose, since our lives are inextricably linked to the lives of others, that it's any choice at all.

"Can they treat it?"

"They can try."

"So there's a chance?"

"With chemo, I might have a couple years. Depends. It started in the prostate," he says, "but it's spread to the bones and liver."

I turn off the highway and onto the road that leads to his house. The pines here, along the shady side of the mountain, have fared better. There is undergrowth and grasses beneath them and their needles are still green.

"You know you have to tell them," I say.

Nick looks away. He stares out the window and then something inside him breaks and the words come, not fast or anxiously, but evenly, steadily, how he doesn't think Joan can handle it, how she *depends* on him, how she *needs* him and that it's not dying, no, not dying so much as how she'll get by, how the girls will get by when he's not around, when he can't bring home a check. That's what scares him. He can't *afford* to die. They live month to month and the first thing to go will be the house. Then the cars. Or maybe it's the other way around. Who knows? He's confused and that's why he wants to talk to me because Joan is fragile and he fears this will break her. He doesn't want them to have to see it, either, the withering, the weakening as the cancer eats him up from the inside out so that his breath stinks of it, and he goes on like this until I put my hand on his shoulder and tell him that he's wrong. About them having to watch. My father, I say, died of cancer and I didn't care how he looked. Of course I didn't want to see him in pain, and of course it was heartbreaking, but none of it made any difference because I loved him just as your children and wife love you. It's about time and only time and so far as what Joan can or can't handle is not for you to decide. She needs to know as do your daughters, so they can make their own decisions.

You owe them that, I say, and from here on out you have to take it a day at a time, like we do as drunks, only now it is a different, more insidious disease. Alcoholism can be arrested, but when stage-four cancer metastasizes its progression is ultimately unstoppable.

We've reached his house. I pull into the driveway but he doesn't get out, not right away. He's still staring out the window.

"You okay?" I say.

He nods and it's understood that while one burden has been lifted another has taken its place. This, too, will be lifted when he speaks to his wife.

"I'll pick you up at six thirty," I say.

"You sure it's no trouble?"

"I'm sure."

Many homes in Lake Arrowhead are built on steep mountain slopes. A long flight of stairs takes you up to Nick's house, and I watch him climb them with deliberation. In the months ahead, as he begins to weaken, these stairs will become more difficult for him. I will watch my friend use the tools of prayer and meditation and a belief in a Power greater than himself. I will watch him use the very things he taught me.

Now Nick reaches the door. Now his wife steps out onto the

porch to greet him. They kiss. Then she looks down at me, sitting in my car in the driveway, waiting. Waiting. Even from this distance I can see that she is smiling at me. It isn't in me to return her smile. But she waves, too, and I can do that. I can wave back.

The Call

The meeting has just started when Nick pulls out his cell phone. He looks at the screen. We're sitting next to each other in steel fold-out chairs, and I can see it's a text message, but I can't make out what it says. He nudges me with his elbow, then leans in close, keeping his voice low.

"C'mon," he says, "we have to go."

This is the morning after New Year's and the place is packed with locals and tourists and newcomers who very likely, after a bout of hard partying the night before, made resolutions to swear off the bottle once and for all. Some of them are still drunk or terribly hungover. The odor of stale alcohol hangs in the air. Nick and I are in the center of the middle row, so it takes some maneuvering to get to the aisle. Someone is reading aloud "How It Works" and a cranky woman gives me a dirty look when I accidently bump her knee trying to slip by her. Outside Nick tells me what's going on. This is about a year before he learns that he has cancer, though he must've already had the ugly seed of it growing inside him, metastasizing as we speak.

"You know Johnny D.?"

I shake my head. I'm terrible with names and it's only getting worse with age.

"The carpet guy?" he says.

That jogs my memory.

"Yeah," I say.

Johnny of Johnny's Carpet Cleaning. His name and business is written in wavy script on the side of a van I've noticed a few times in the parking lot outside our A.A. club. But I don't recall seeing that van or Johnny at a meeting in quite a while. So many people come in and out of the rooms of A.A. that nobody could possibly keep track of them all.

Nick claps me on the back.

"Well," he says, "you're going on your first Twelfth Step call, buddy."

At the time I'm only one year and eight months sober and don't feel qualified to be rescuing drunks, which is what a Twelfth Step call is about. If they're halfway coherent, you do your best to convince them of the severity of their problem, and usually, since they called for help in the first place, they're willing to listen. You want to get them when they're most vulnerable and remorseful, when they're hungover, feeling sick and lousy and full of regret. You want them to vow not to drink, at least for today. Then you take them to a meeting right away. Sooner the better. I tell Nick I don't feel too confident about this, trying to save a drunk with so little sober time under my belt. It's a job for more experienced members of A.A.

"Even if you only had one day," he says, "it's one day more than this poor bastard. Besides, it's not about time. It's about being there for another drunk when he needs you." He unlocks the car door for me and I get in. He slides in on his side and starts the engine. "This isn't my first Twelfth Step call with this guy. 'Sometimes quickly, sometimes slowly . . .'" he says, quoting from the Big Book about how sobriety comes quickly for some and slowly, if ever, for others. "Either way we don't give up. Put on your seat belt."

Johnny lives in a nice two-story house in a middle-class neighborhood in Lake Arrowhead. But the front yard is over-grown with weeds, and the house's paint is chipped in spots along the eaves and around the windows. One of the glass panes in the front door is broken out and covered with cardboard. A van is parked at an odd angle in the driveway. Nick and I get out of the car and walk up to the porch. He rings the bell. There's no answer. He looks at me and rings it again. Again there's no answer. He reaches for the doorknob and turns it. It's unlocked. Nick goes in first but I'm right behind him, and we don't have to go far to find the guy, just past the foyer, in the living room where he's passed out on the couch.

Fortunately he's lying on his side, so he didn't choke on his vomit, because there's a mess of it on the cushion beside his head. He's wet his pants, too, but the hardest part is seeing his little boy, maybe seven or eight, curled up in the lounge chair next to him, playing a video game on the TV. The sound is off so as not to disturb his father, I'm guessing, though in his state it wouldn't have mattered. The little boy is wearing Ninja Turtles pajamas. He has big round eyes, and I remember looking into them, as he looks at us, before he returns his attention to the game. That really gets me. How two strangers coming into his home doesn't even faze the kid. And his ears! I've never seen anything like them. They stick straight out from his head. I looked it up later and it's a condition, a deformity, commonly known as *bat ears*. Imagine the teasing and ridicule he gets at school. Combine that with a drunk for a father, and apparently no mother to take up the slack, and it's easy to see why the kid prefers to reside in the world of video games rather than the messed-up one around him.

I'd say Johnny is in his early thirties, but the drinking life ages you, and he looks older. He has thick bags under his eyes and the coarse skin of a heavy smoker. On the coffee table is an empty half gallon of cheap Popov vodka, an empty pack of Camels, an ashtray full of butts, and the cell phone he used to text Nick, apparently before he passed out. Nick scoots Johnny's legs back to make a spot to sit.

"Johnny," he says. "*Johnny*. Wake up."

That doesn't do it, so Nick shakes him a little. Slowly Johnny's eyes open. Slowly it dawns on him, who he's looking at. I doubt he remembers texting Nick. The first time he tries to sit up, he falls back on the couch, but on the second attempt he makes it.

"I'm sorry," he says.

I know those words all too well. I've said them myself so many times to so many others in circumstances very much like this one.

"You have nothing to be sorry about. You're an alcoholic," Nick says, "just doing what us alcoholics do best. But we're here for you, man."

Johnny puts his elbows on his knees and hides his face in his hands and then it pours out, tears and all, admitting how he needs help. How he knows it's killing him but he can't quit. How he hates himself. How he loves his son and doesn't want to lose him.

His feelings run from fear and frustration and sadness to anger, hopelessness, despair, and self-pity all rolled into one painful outburst. I look at the kid. He hasn't missed a beat playing his video game. It's as if he hasn't heard a word, and that gets me again, how he's able to shut it all out. Shut it all down. After a while, when the sobbing subsides, Nick pats him on the back.

"Let's get you to a meeting."

"Right now?"

"After you shower and change," he says. "We can't bring you like this."

Johnny looks at his son.

"What about Hunter?"

"What about him?"

"I can't leave him alone."

"He can come with us." Nick nods at me. "Jim will look after him."

"It's no problem. It's no big deal," I say. "I have three boys myself."

Johnny tells him to put on some clothes, and when he heads for his room, we help his father up off the couch and guide him down the hallway, one of us on each side, so we can catch him in case he falls. In the bathroom, he has trouble getting his pants off and keeping his balance, so Nick puts the lid down on the toilet seat and makes him sit first. The last thing we want is him slipping and cracking his head. He can't get his fingers to unbutton his shirt, they're shaking too much, so I help him.

He looks at me.

"Pretty pathetic when you can't unbutton your own fucking shirt."

"Hey," I say, "one time I was up at Deep Creek. You know how steep the trails are there. I bent over to tie my shoe and I was so plastered I went right over the side. Must've fell ten, fifteen feet. I'm lucky I didn't kill myself."

"No shit?"

"No shit," I say. "I was pretty bruised up but I didn't break a bone."

It isn't true, the story I tell him, but if it makes him feel better, I don't see the harm. He showers and changes, and soon, at least from appearances, he's presentable in Levi's and a V-neck sweater and some suede slip-ons. Hunter does a good job getting himself ready, except that he has his T-shirt turned inside out. "Better grab a jacket," Nick tells him, before we leave. It's the tail end of winter, and it's chilly, forty degrees tops today.

The meeting runs two hours, and by the time we get back, it's more than half over. That means I'm in charge of looking after Hunter for the next thirty or forty minutes. There's a Rite Aid drugstore in the shopping complex across from our A.A. club, and to escape the cold I figure we can kill some time browsing the aisles. I buy him a box of Hot Tamales and a Hulk Hogan action figure. I get a pack of cigarettes for myself.

Outside the store, while I'm lighting up, we hear sirens. They get louder and louder, and then there it is, an ambulance, pulling up in front of the A.A. club. Two paramedics jump out and rush inside. In no time a small crowd from the Rite Aid gathers in the parking lot and they're all staring. If I'd had any sense I would've taken the kid's hand and led him in the opposite direction, so he never would've had to see his father wheeled out on a stretcher, one shoe missing. If I'd had any sense I might've reacted more quickly and kept this memory, this image, from being imprinted on the young boy's mind. But I'm caught up in the moment and don't think fast enough.

I expect Hunter to run after his father. I expect to have to grab him. I expect him to shout or scream or burst into tears. But none of these things happen. Instead he stares at the ground, and after the ambulance leaves and the crowd disperses, he sits down on a nearby bench. He opens the bag from the Rite Aid and takes out the Hulk Hogan action figure and starts working the arms around. I understand his reaction. I have a boy around his age who once witnessed me have an alcoholic breakdown at the dinner table and quietly got up and took his plate over to the couch and turned on the TV. I'll never forget that. It's a sad and pathetic thing when the innocent child becomes accustomed to the insanities of the parent.

Having someone carted out on a stretcher during a meeting would ordinarily be grounds for adjourning early. But the members of A.A. are not ordinary. Most of us are used to seeing the inside of ambulances and jails, blacking out or wrecking cars, and when we're trading war stories in a meeting, we'll often laugh at such things where others would naturally recoil in horror. Or disgust. Hell or high water that meeting continues, and I sit there with Hunter until it's over, all as if nothing unusual has happened. Finally Nick and the others come out the door. I can see him looking around for me, so I wave to him. He spots me and we walk toward each other across the parking lot. Hunter, he's still playing with his Hulk Hogan, and he can't hear us. We're too far away.

"What happened?" I say.

"He passed out. Just fell out of his chair right onto the floor and started to seize."

"Jesus Christ."

"Jesus Christ is right," Nick says. "He was twitching and convulsing all over."

"You think he'll be okay?"

"I think so. He was starting to come out of it when the paramedics got here." Nick reaches into his pocket and hands me a cell phone. This is back in the day of flip-tops when you didn't need a password to get into somebody's phone. "It's Johnny's. Hang on to it. I called his parents and they're on their way now. Can you look after Hunter a little longer? They're driving in from Indio, so it'll be a couple hours. I want to be at the hospital when Johnny comes to and see if I can't get him to check himself into rehab." Nick glances at the kid sitting on the bench outside the Rite Aid. "He'll lose that boy if he doesn't clean up."

I'm surprised he hasn't lost him already, but I don't say it. I ask about the boy's mother. Nick shakes his head.

"No," he says, "she's worse off than him. That's why the kid lives with Johnny."

With time to kill I drive Hunter over to Lake Arrowhead Village where there are restaurants and outlet stores and souvenir shops. I tell him that his grandparents are on their way to pick him up, that they'll be here soon, and while we're waiting we go to McDonald's and I get him a Happy Meal. I buy myself a Big Mac. We take the warm bags down to the lake and sit on the bank. It's not a huge lake, maybe a couple miles long, but the water is clear and blue and it's nice to look at. The shoreline across from us is cluttered with expensive homes. Most are unoccupied, second homes for wealthy people from LA and Orange County who only use them in the summer or on winter holidays. In among the houses are tall pines and beyond them are mountains and more trees. Our breath is white in the cold air and the wind off the lake makes my eyes water.

"You go to Grandview?" I say. Grandview is one of the elementary schools up here.

"Yeah," he says.

"What grade?"

"Second."

"I got a little boy in fourth. Nate Brown. Do you know him?"

He doesn't say anything and I let it go at that. Soon a momma duck spots us eating and swims over with seven baby ducklings trailing her in a straight row. That's enough to get a smile out of anybody, but not this kid, at least not today. But he still feeds them, tearing pieces off his hamburger bun and tossing them into the water. I do the same.

Hunter doesn't look at me.

"Is he dying?"

"What?"

"My dad, is he dying? You can tell me," he says. "I'm old enough."

These are not the words of a child, and they startle me, how plainly and emotionlessly he speaks of something so absolute as death. Maybe, as a way of steeling himself, he's considered it a real possibility for his father many times before. I'm guessing he has, and it makes me wonder about my own boys, if I worried them like this. I'm sure I did, and it pains me. I wish it were different but I know it is not.

"I have a right to know," he says.

I try to put my arm around him but he's not having it. He pulls away.

"Your dad is fine," I tell him. "He just drank too much and passed out. They called the ambulance because they couldn't wake him up. But he's not dying. Don't think like that. He's going to be okay."

He looks down at the dirt, then out across the lake. I think for a second.

"You know how to skip rocks?"

He doesn't say anything.

I pick up a rock and throw it sidearm across the lake. It bounces along the surface three times before it sinks. I do it again. Four skips this time. I catch him looking. "Give it a try," I say. He acts like he's not interested, but after some coaxing, if only to shut me up, he looks around for a rock. On his first two throws the rocks hit the water and go straight down.

"This is stupid," he says.

"You just have to get the hang of it," I say.

I tell him that he wants a flat rock, the flattest he can find, and then I show him how to hold it, between his thumb and index finger. "Let your wrist do the work," I tell him. I demonstrate how you lean over and fling it from your waist, from the side, so your arm is parallel to the water. He gives it another try and this one sails out across the lake, skipping once, twice, three times.

"There you go," I say, "now that's a throw."

I think I detect a smile. Then Johnny's cell phone rings. It's Hunter's grandmother. She's waiting on us at the Rite Aid, and I tell her we'll be there in ten minutes. The boy throws another rock. It skips three times. Those crazy ears of his are bright red from the cold.

She's standing outside the doors of the Rite Aid when we get there. Her hair is gray and made up into a bob and she's wearing a faded Levi's jacket, jeans, and boots. As we approach, the grandfather slips out from behind the wheel of a Ford pickup parked nearby and comes over and shakes my hand. He wears a straw cowboy hat. There are a couple bales of hay in the back, so I'm guessing they own a small ranch in the desert of Indio. He thanks me for my troubles, and I tell him it's no trouble at all. She thanks me, too, and when she bends down and hugs the boy, he hugs her back. They seem like decent people. I like to think that he'll be okay.

I like to think that his father will be okay, too. I like to think that he's hit his last bottom and won't drink anymore. I like to think that the next time the boy goes to the lake it'll be with his father and they'll feed the ducks together and skip rocks. Then I think of my youngest, Nate, and I don't remember ever taking him to the lake to feed the ducks and skip rocks. I promise myself I will, and I do, the following week. We have a fine time, just the two of us, and later when I tell Nick about it, he says that's one of the gifts of sobriety, how we come to appreciate lives other than our own.

Fast-forward about eight months.

I haven't seen Johnny or his son since that day. Talk around the A.A. circle is that he moved off the mountain and into a halfway house in San Bernardino after he left rehab. Another rumor is that he'd moved back home with his parents in Indio. I don't know how much if any of it is true, but I'm doing some shopping at our local grocery store when I spot him and Hunter in the aisle with the breakfast cereals. Those bat ears, they aren't sticking out anymore. He must've had them worked on, and recently, because behind each ear is a thin strip of white gauze. And Johnny looks younger, thinner, no alcoholic bloat. It's summer and he has on a tank top and his shoulders are sunburned. The boy wears shorts and flip-flops and he looks sunburned, too. I'd say, by the looks of them, that they've been down at the lake swimming. Maybe fishing. Hunter is pushing the cart. He stops and pulls a box of Lucky Charms off the shelf.

"Can I have these?"

"How about the Honey Nut Cheerios?" Johnny says. "You like those. They're healthier."

"I'm tired of Cheerios."

"Put it back," he says, but when the boy starts to do as he's told, Johnny sees the disappointment in his eyes and has a change of heart.

"Okay, okay. But next time it's Cheerios."

Hunter smiles. I thought I'd detected a faint smile from him at the lake some eight months earlier when he skipped his first rock, but there is no mistaking this one. Neither of them notices me watching, and I'd like to say hello, but it's better this way. Seeing me would only take them back to a place that I'm sure they would prefer not to go. I push my cart past them and continue down the aisle.

Iron

With a few hundred pounds of iron hovering over me, I don't think about drinking. I don't think about using. I am lying on my back doing a bench press, and in lowering the barbell to my chest and pushing it back up, I am in a state of no-mindedness, otherwise known as Zen.

I cannot hesitate.

I cannot doubt.

I cannot worry. I cannot dwell on my many failures in life. I cannot feel the guilt or remorse or regret that frequently plagues me, even after years of being sober. I envision no gruesome images. I cannot project into the future any further than the immediate moment at hand. I cannot, in short, *think*.

All I can do is react to the weight pushing down on me with man's most basic human instinct to survive. It is pure. It is primal. It is fight or flight but flight is not an option once the bar is lifted from the rack. Adrenaline spikes. The iron is a threat that must be met with more than the power it exerts. Resistance equal to that power only stabilizes it, and muscle, like best intentions, weakens in stasis. A thing in a state of uniform motion will remain in that state unless an external force acts on it. This is one of Newton's laws of motion, and I compare it to the compulsion to drink. And I compare the compulsion to drink to the simple act of lowering and raising a barbell, and how, if I do not push back harder than it pushes on me, it will prevail. Iron, for this drunk, is about salvation and sanity.

In those few seconds, as the weight bears down on me, I cease to exist.

I am not in recovery.

I am recovered.

Other alcoholic-addicts find a similar state of reprieve in yoga or Pilates. I have a writer friend in LA that fanatically runs six miles a day, five days a week, whether it's a hundred degrees out or pouring rain. Physical exertion takes me out of myself. It gets those endorphins going. It resensitizes the same neurotransmitters responsible for a sense of well-being that as an alcoholic-addict I overstimulated and desensitized with drugs and booze.

Each time I slip beneath a heavy weight, I am testing myself. I am relearning what should be permanently etched in my mind. The weight could crush me. The weight could prevail. There are consequences for the risks I take, which is something I could not have cared less about when I was stoned out of my head, wandering through dangerous neighborhoods late at night searching for more of the substances that would keep me from my head. I like being reminded of that, who I was and where I came from, because it's easy to forget. Easy to think I'm safe. As if I'm all better now.

Complacency, they say, kills.

The same time and attention I put into getting high is not

unlike the time and attention required of me to get clean and sober and stay that way.

I work out two to three hours a day, five, sometimes six days a week, and over the years my body weight has gone from a tweaker-thin 150 to a solid 190. I've heard psychologists claim that it's not so much alcohol and drugs that alcoholic-addicts have to worry about as it is their obsessive behavior. That it's obsession itself that people like me really need to confront and overcome to be mentally healthy. And maybe they have a point. But in the meantime, until I get that part figured out, I'd argue that I best be left to my own devices. The neurotic compulsion to exercise is, in my estimation, a tad less harmful than drinking, popping pills, or sticking a needle in my arm.

I am lying on the bench press now.

The bar itself weighs forty-five pounds and on each side of it are three forty-five-pound iron plates. The total is 315 pounds. Gripping the bar, hands about shoulder width apart, I take a deep breath.

Hold it.

Arch my back. Lift.

I feel the pressure of the weight move through my arms down into my chest. I am not thinking. It is just me and the iron and the iron is inert and lifeless.

In lowering it toward my chest, I feel my muscles contract and harden, and I like the feeling. This sense of power flowing through my body. I push the weight back up and do it again. I do it until I can barely do another. Then I return it to the rack. I let my arms down and rest a short while. Once I've caught my breath, I grip the bar again.

Arch my back. Lift.

Another one of Newton's laws of motion is that for every action there is an equal and opposite reaction. To build muscle, I have to first tear the muscle down, and to tear the muscle down means I can't stop lifting until I reach failure. I can't stop until there is nothing left in me to give. And there is always more to give, if not today, then another day, when I push beyond the simple limits of the body to a further, more distant place where failure becomes the source of a strength greater than any I could ever find in the physical world.

This Little Girl

She keeps coming back, this little girl. I'm six years old. She's eight, nine tops, and she's riding her bike. It's a Schwinn Sting-Ray with red streamers on the handlebars. I'm thinking maybe it's a birthday present, partly because it looks shiny and brand-new, and partly because she's excited in the way I've seen my own children become when they've received a special gift. It's that or she's just learned to ride the bike, and after many falls and scrapes, she's finally found her balance, keeping the wheel straight, feeling the wind in her face, and she's happy and proud as she coasts down the driveway. She's wearing a light-blue summer dress. She has pigtails. She's smiling and her teeth seem extraordinarily white against the blackness of her skin.

Over the years I repressed the memory, shoving it back into the darkest corners of the mind, another item amid the clutter of the many things I would rather not remember. We didn't know each other. I never knew her name. She was a child, like me, growing up in a poor neighborhood in East San Jose, and God knows there were plenty of us. It was block after block of run-down apartments where families were always moving in or moving out. I like to tell myself that I have no reason to remember her, and yet here I am, sixty years old, writing about a little girl on a bicycle who is smiling as she coasts down the driveway and into the street when the car hits her.

It's a white lowrider. I believe it's a Chevy and it doesn't stop. Doesn't even slow down. But it swerves farther down the road and scrapes the side of a parked car. It swerves again as it takes a wide sloppy turn at the end of the street and disappears. I don't think about it then, that the driver is drunk, but I will later when I'm much older and sober and realize how fortunate I am not to have killed or injured anyone in the thousands of times I've driven drunk. Children, it seems, are the greatest casualties of the reck- lessness of alcoholics and addicts, and I want to believe that those days are behind me. I hope so, anyway. But that car, that Chevy lowrider, it keeps going, and it's still going as I write this story, speeding down the road, passing through the years.

Paula, my wife, she's learned to read me. She can sense when I'm distant, when I'm too quiet, and she'll ask what's wrong. Usu- ally I say I'm fine. Just tired. But she can be persistent, and so sometimes I tell her the truth, and sometimes the truth has to do with this little girl. It happens again the other night at Farmer Boys over hamburgers, and when I tell her what I'm thinking about, the little girl and *those eyes, those eyes,* my wife says that whether I know it or not I've been traumatized.

"You never used to think about her or at least you didn't tell me. But lately," she says, "and by lately I mean *years,* it's been happening way too much. Maybe you should see someone. Talk about it."

That someone is a shrink, and I have my reservations about shrinks. The few I've known are too quick to prescribe meds, as if there's a chemical answer to all life's ills. Just because the little girl refuses to be ignored doesn't mean I've been psychologically damaged. *Traumatized* is a strong word. Maybe some things can't be fixed, assuming they're even broken, somehow for the worst, and I'm not so sure that's the case here. Maybe some things, like the memory of this little girl, should be embraced. Held near and dear. Maybe it should be played over and over in the mind, so if something like it were to ever happen again on my watch, I could get it right. I could learn. And I like to think I do, when I rewind the tape in my head, so it happens like this:

I am six years old. She is eight or nine. She is wearing a light-blue summer dress. She has pigtails and she's smiling brightly as she coasts down the driveway on her bike and into the street when the car hits her.

A half dozen of us stand watching from the curb. We'd been playing. What game I don't recall. The other children are all faceless to me now but the girl I see clearly. She lies on her back on the hot pavement. She has green eyes and she is looking up at the sky, but I don't think she sees anything. I am amazed at the length of her intestines and how they uncoil along the asphalt, snakelike, stretching across the street. I am amazed at how glossy they are, how they gleam in the sun, and I wonder how is it possible that something so long could fit inside something so small as this body.

Down the block an old Mexican man steadies himself on a cane. He is watching, too, and when another car approaches, he steps into the street and waves his arms over his head for the driver to stop. He shouts at us. This is long before the day of cell phones.

"Go home," he says. "Tell your parents to call an ambulance. Hurry. Run."

I don't remember any of us leaving. Instead I move closer to the little girl, slowly, until I am only a few feet away. She is looking up at the sky and saying "momma . . . momma." There are tiny beads of sweat on her forehead, just beneath her hairline, and I want somehow to help but I do nothing, and I believe it is this that most troubles me. As an adult it is easy to rationalize. What could a six-year-old possibly have done? The child is blameless, and yet the child, watching another child die, believes otherwise.

So I do now, in a story, what I wish I'd done in life.

Memory is my only offering, and I get down on my knees. I slip my fingers under the base of her neck, so that her head is off the hot asphalt, and I cradle her body to my chest. She is looking into the sky, and when she says "momma . . . momma," I say, gently, over and over, "I'm here, baby, I'm here." She is in shock. She doesn't know if I am her mother or not and I like to believe it does not matter. When the little girl returns to me, I like to believe, as I watch the light go out of her eyes, that holding her is what the remembering has always been about.

The Motions

The prison I visit is only a few miles from Interstate 15. It is the deadliest highway in the United States, and the surrounding land, far as you can see, is flat and dry and desolate. Sagebrush is about all that grows here and even it is sparse. Summers hit 110 or better. Winters bring torrential rains and dangerous floods, but the highway itself is straight and well paved, no sudden twists or turns; the road is not the cause of the many collisions and casualties. Blame rests squarely on the shoulders of the drivers, most rushing to Vegas, anxious to test their luck. Others are returning home, hungover from the night before, guilt-ridden and angry for all they've gambled away, and if they're from San Bernardino, it's likely they didn't have it to lose.

We are just behind Detroit as the poorest city in America. Thirty-five percent of the residents live in poverty. Forty-six percent receive welfare, and according to FBI statistics we have the third-highest gang population of any county in the nation. In visiting the prison I am walking into a microcosm of the violent culture that exists outside these walls. San Bernardino is among the top thirty cities in the United States with the highest murder rates. In California, it typically ranks beneath Fresno and Oakland. Aggravated assault is generally more than three times the national average, and robberies and carjackings are so common as to be daily, mundane occurrences. Wherever you are in this city, but especially at night, you best watch your back.

I go with a friend, Sam, armed with books and literature from Alcoholics Anonymous, a stack of court cards, and schedules of support meetings for those soon to be released. We are armed, too, with a belief that we can make a difference in the lives of these men. But it is a fragile belief. We are veterans of a guerrilla war that can't be won and we steel ourselves against the overwhelming odds of helping others help themselves. We cling to the hope that we'll connect with a handful of the hundreds we've seen in our many visits. We cling to the hope that we're planting the seed for change and we keep our expectations low. Sometimes, it seems, we're just going through the motions.

These men remind us of who we were and where we've been and who we could so easily become again if we take our sobriety for granted. Sam is a former infantryman, and when he returned from Vietnam he took a job as a carney, traveling with a circus across the country, pumped up on speed and booze for nearly twenty years, until, finally, inevitably, he crashed and burned. First thing they did, when he checked himself into rehab at the VA, was pull all his teeth. Meth had rotted them black to the root. Now in his midfifties he works in the produce section of a grocery store and attends seminary two nights a week. He's studying to be a pastor, but I've never seen him impose his religious beliefs on anyone.

I admire him for that.

I admire him also for speaking regularly to youth groups, serving meals to the homeless at the Salvation Army, leading meetings at A.A., sponsoring and mentoring other alcoholics and addicts, all while pulling down forty plus hours a week at the grocery store. The same dedication holds true for Tod, another friend and devoted member of A.A. who often accompanies us, but he is taking a well-deserved vacation this month, gone fishing in Idaho.

I take this commitment on the advice of my sponsor after I reach my first year of sobriety. Because I did my Fifth Step with him, because he knows about the crimes I committed as a teenager, Nick thinks I'm a perfect candidate for the job. "Since you have some solid time under your belt," he says, "you need to start helping others, especially those in a place you could've wound up yourself." And so, though I'm nervous about it, feeling that a year clean hardly qualifies me as any sort of authority on sobriety, I now find myself meeting Sam in the parking lot at the prison on Friday nights twice a month. It's usually ten to fifteen degrees warmer in the flatlands of San Bernardino than it is where we live in the mountains, and given that I'm used to the cooler climate, it feels warm this autumn night. I'm early, with ten minutes to spare, so I light up a cigarette and then empty my pockets into the glove compartment. A lock-blade knife sharp enough to shave the hair on my arm. Nickels and dimes and pennies. A Bic lighter. I remove my driver's license and stow my wallet, too. All we're allowed to take into the prison, aside from our A.A. literature, is the key to our car. Our licenses, we turn them over to the guard before entering.

Smog does stunning things to the sky when the sun sets, filling it with swirls of orange, yellow, blue, and faint shades of purple, and while I'm leaning against my car, smoking and taking in the beautiful desert skyline, Sam drives into the lot. We each grab a cardboard box stuffed with literature from the bed of his truck and walk to the guard's booth. The officer working behind the bulletproof glass has seen us so often that he collects our licenses, slips our name tags through the same slot, and buzzes us through the steel gate without a word. Once the first gate locks behind us, he buzzes open the second.

Twenty-foot-high chain-link fences topped with barbed wire protect the entire perimeter of the prison. The first time I came here, I expected to find the same dirt, sand, and rock inside the prison grounds as the land that surrounds it, but instead it was as if I'd entered a meticulously well-kept park. The sprawling green lawns are neatly mown and perfectly edged. The hanging branches of the many elm trees are uniformly pruned and cut to match the others. Randomly spaced around the grounds are aluminum picnic benches, and the walkways are carefully swept, the concrete white and clean. It's all the more impressive because this prison opened a half century ago, and though originally designed to hold a hundred male inmates, through the years, with expansion and remodeling, it now houses over a thousand. An adjacent facility is home to three hundred women.

But for all the neatly groomed lawns, trees, and spotless walkways, there's no mistaking what this place is about. As Sam and I make our way to the main dorm, we pass the exercise yard for the maximum security unit, nicknamed "The Pumpkin Patch." The general prison population is issued blue, hospital-style scrubs, but the ones here must wear bright-orange jumpsuits, identifying them as having committed more heinous crimes, and so they are also more strictly confined. Their exercise yard is a chain-link cage with a basketball court, two pull-up bars, another for dips, and it's noisy. It's loud. The cage is full of young men and they're shouting and laughing. Some shoot hoops. Some toss around a football. Others wait in line to use the pull-up and dip bars, but most lean against the walls, talking and joking. A tall lanky kid stands by himself away from the crowds, and I catch his eye. He's staring me down, and I can feel it, his anger. I'd smile if I didn't think it would set him off, but anything short of looking away is pointless.

They self-segregate. Brown with brown. Black with black. White with white. The majority is brown, followed by black, and the whites, maybe a dozen, are in the corner of the yard. They're in formation, one straight row, on the ground, doing push-ups. An older inmate, I'm guessing around forty, paces back and forth in front of the line. His head is shaved. His neck and arms are heavily tatted.

"Thirty-one," he shouts, "thirty-two, thirty-three . . ."

A former student of mine could've been that lanky kid staring me down or one of those in the formation doing push-ups. He was in The Pumpkin Patch for two years, this student, and he wrote me a letter, sent it to the university, and in it he asked if I could visit him. He was young and thought highly of me and he used to drop by during my office hours to talk about stories and writing. There was a depth and maturity to his work that I rarely see from the students in my classes, and as we came to know each other better he confided in me that he had a problem with methamphetamine and alcohol, it was why he sometimes missed class or turned in a late assignment. I confided in him that I understood. That I struggled myself and had started going to A.A. I kept falling short, but I'd collect clean time, thirty days here or there, sometimes longer, often less, and then, inevitably it seemed, I'd backslide. His pattern was the same as mine, and we'd talk about it, encourage each other, but when he wrote me from prison I was going through a divorce and drinking and using heavily. I threw his letter in my office trash can. I couldn't think about him. I couldn't think about anybody or anything but myself and where my next drink or drug was coming from. I think of him now, though, and it is with guilt and regret for failing to honor the simple request of a former student when he needed me most.

Sam and I reach the dorms, the medium security facility, and again we're stopped by a guard. The front door is open and the noise spills out. Shouting. Talking. Laughter. A couple hundred men are housed in here.

Sam has to raise his voice.

"We're with A.A.," he says. "You want us to meet the guys inside or out tonight, sir?"

"You picked a lousy time," the guard says.

It's our regular time. It's our regular day. If it's a lousy time, then why weren't we told earlier at the main gate? But I keep my mouth shut. We need to stay on good terms with the guards, always addressing them as *sir*, and never complaining, or even asking for a reason if they want us to leave. Our being here is a privilege, not a right, and it can be revoked at any time. Through the open door I see a long row of prisoners, all stripped to the waist, lined up against the wall. One guard watches while another wearing latex gloves goes from inmate to inmate, carefully running his hands up and down their legs.

"You want us to cancel?"

"Hang on, let me call the sergeant first. Why don't you guys wait in the yard," he says. "I'll let you know what's up in a minute."

We walk back to the yard and set the boxes of literature on the grass and take a seat at one of the picnic benches.

"Something's going down," I say.

"They're probably looking for a shank."

"Or dope."

"They might kick us out if they don't find it, whatever it is. Tell you the truth," Sam says, "I wouldn't mind. I'm exhausted tonight."

"I don't know how you do it," I say. "Working and going to seminary school and hitting meetings and then all this volunteer stuff."

"Shit," he says. "I spent a lot more time getting fucked up in bars and dope houses than I ever did trying to help anybody."

Between getting wasted, thinking about getting wasted, tracking down the stuff that gets you wasted, and recuperating from being wasted so we could get wasted again, Sam and I are neck and neck in throwing our lives away. Like me, he burned through a marriage and lost precious sober and sane years when he should have been raising his kids.

The guard at the dorms shouts to the inmates.

"A.A. outside . . . A.A. outside."

So the meeting is on. Sam and I drag two picnic benches together and unpack the boxes. We set out stacks of paperback Big Books, A.A. schedules for inmates with release dates coming up, court cards for ones busted for narcotics, multiple DUIs, or both, and a bunch of different pamphlets on alcoholism, including one called *A.A. for Prisoners.*

Sometimes only a handful show.

Sometimes we get a dozen or so. But tonight, maybe because of the pat down, the prisoners need to cool off, need to get away from the guards for a while, and so they swarm us. It's the biggest crowd we've ever had, and for the next ten minutes all I do is sign court cards, fill out ones for new inmates, and sign those, too. They'll need them as evidence of their willingness to stay clean and sober when they go for their parole hearings. Whether they're sincere or not is anyone's guess.

Sam hands out pamphlets and Big Books.

"Who needs a Spanish edition?" he says. We only have a few and they go quick.

Prisoners are fanned out across the yard. Some sit with their legs crossed. Some stretch out on the grass, heads propped up on one elbow. Others stand with their arms folded over their chest. They're all dressed in blue scrubs. The top is a V-neck, and you can see the T-shirts they wear underneath with their prison call numbers written in black felt pen along the collar. As usual they group together according to race. This I expect, but two things that always strike me, no matter how many times I visit here, is the age of the inmates and how they've inked themselves. The majority are in their twenties, some their teens, and nearly all have shaved heads marred with tattoos. Many have inked their faces, too.

Cheeks.

Chins.

Foreheads. One young man has *Fuck You, Motherfucker* written across his neck in Old English–style lettering. I don't see this kid working at McDonald's anytime soon.

Sam nudges me.

"You want to lead tonight?"

"Sure."

I read out loud the first part of the A.A. Preamble, then call on a prisoner to read the second part. When he's done, I look into the crowd.

"My name is Jim," I say, "and I'm an alcoholic."

Many of the prisoners are familiar with the A.A. drill, that the leader shares his story first, and that they're supposed to repeat my name in unison.

"Hey, Jim," they say.

Wearing blue scrubs means they're medium security inmates, and although most are drug and alcohol offenders, they know as well as I do that you only do time for the crime you're busted for. And not by a long shot does that mean you didn't commit a whole bunch of others before then. Who knows how many belong in The Pumpkin Patch?

Someone in the back shouts.

"Yo, dog, you yolked. How much you bench?"

Some of the men laugh.

"Three-twenty on a good day," I say. "Let me see a show of hands. Who here's done something illegal, B&E, strong-arm, whatever, when you were wasted? I'm talking something you wouldn't have done if you *weren't* fucked up?"

A young man on the sidelines raises his hand. Another looks around the crowd and then slowly, tentatively, does the same.

Soon, of the thirty or so here, most of them are holding their hands up.

I raise mine too.

I tell them a small part of my story, crime-wise, mostly just burglaries when I'm a kid, and where it starts for me with drugs, when I'm nine with marijuana. Booze comes at twelve and by fourteen it's everything and anything I can get my hands on. But it's meth, I add, that delivers the knockout blow in my forties. "I probably had a few more years of drinking left in me," I say, "if I didn't come across that shit." I tell them, too, about my brother and sister drinking and killing themselves, my mother doing hard time, and my father, for the most part, MIA as I'm growing up. The idea is to be open and honest so that they feel more comfortable being open and honest when I ask them to share. I don't expect them to talk about their crimes. I just want to drive home the connection between drinking and using and the fucked-up choices we make because of it.

"Let's open this meeting up," I say.

I point to a Hispanic kid sitting in the middle of the group.

"You got something to say?"

He has three dots tattooed in a triangle under the corner of his eye. It can mean any number of things, from the harmless *mi vida loca* to a symbol of those firmly committed to thug life, representing the three places gang members openly and proudly accept as their fate. Time in prison. Time in hospitals. Or an early grave.

"I'll pass, man."

I nod to the guy next to him.

"How about you?"

He has *909* tatted on his forehead. San Bernardino area code. Not the best tat if he bumps into the wrong gentlemen in the 213, downtown LA.

"Fuck it, why not? I'm Rafael and I'm an alcoholic and an addict. I started drinking when I was six. My uncles, they used to throw these big-ass parties and it was always 'get me another beer, *mijo*, get me another beer.' So I did, no problem, but I had to take some sips coming back, right, so I wouldn't spill, right." Some of the men grin. "They knew what I was up to and pretty soon everybody'd be laughing. 'Hey, check out little Rafi.' I'd be stumbling and shit. It was cool. I felt special, but fuck, man, that party never ended." He nods at me. "Like you, booze and meth. First time I took a hit of crystal, fucking A, it was on. I was twenty and my *tio* got me in the union, driving forklift. Had a wife, too, but the bitch left me." He shrugs. "Can't blame her. I was bringing in big bucks and smoking and drinking it all away. She's banging some other dude now, and I don't care, seriously, because you know what hurts, what really hurts? Today's my baby girl's birthday. And where am I? In the fucking *la penta*. She's three and I ain't seen her since she was two months."

He's quiet.

That's the cue for the group to applaud in support and empathy, and most do, though many remain stone-faced. Showing emotion is a sign of weakness, and for Rafael to pour his heart out probably disgusts them.

Sam calls to him.

"Hey, when do you get out?"

"In twenty-two days."

"Where you going?"

"Back to Hesperia," he says, "and I'm scared, homes. I don't want to pick up no more."

Hesperia is a neighboring desert city as well-known as San Bernardino for its poverty, crime, and drugs. Sam takes a pamphlet from the table and hands it to the prisoner standing next to him. It's an A.A. listing of meetings in our desert communities.

"Pass that back to him," he says. Then he looks at Rafael. "First thing you do, first day you're out, is get your ass to a meeting. The chances of staying clean go up about fifty percent if you do, and it's about eighty percent you'll be back here in about a year if you don't."

Where he gets his figures, I have no idea, and whether they're correct or not doesn't really matter. The point is Rafael needs all the support he can get. While you're locked up, your friends don't necessarily stop using and drinking, and when you're released, there's a very good chance they'll want to celebrate your homecoming. All it takes is one drink, one line, one hit off the pipe, and the party that began when Rafael was six can easily pick up right where it left off.

Another prisoner raises his hand.

"I'm Vic and I'm an addict."

This guy is older. I'd say he's in his early forties, and I peg him for a junkie at first sight. He has the classic sunken cheeks and his neck is so thin it makes his head seem abnormally large. But it isn't shaved. I don't see any tats, either. He's probably a fish, what prisoners call a new inmate, because I've seen so many arrive in his condition, skinny and weak, and after a month of regular meals, no dope, and exercise they begin to fill out.

"My girlfriend," he says, "is in the women's block. It was an act of God we were busted. Divine fucking intervention. Heroin is our drug, and we were on a hard run, I mean we were dying, seriously, not eating or drinking, these ugly fucking sores all over, and the thing is we didn't care." Vic is sitting on the lawn and he picks at a blade of grass. "I've been in prison in Mexico and Canada, but never in America. I mean till now. And every time I've been arrested, they always beat the shit out of me. Always. So this last time, when they light me up and I get out of the car, I just cover my head and tell the cop 'go on, get it over with, but please, officer, don't hurt my girl.' And you know what he says? 'Sir, you're so sick I don't even want to touch you. You and your friend need a doctor.' Can you believe he took us straight to the hospital first? The doc told me the abscesses on my left arm were so infected they'd have to amputate if the antibiotics didn't work." He plucks the blade of grass and rolls it between his fingers. "They say God works in mysterious ways and he was working through that cop that day. I owe a *cop* my fucking arm. I owe a *cop* my fucking life. Unbelievable," he says. "Fucking unbelievable." He flicks the blade of grass away like you would a cigarette butt. "My girl and me, if we go on another run, we won't make it back."

A handful of the stone-faced men break from the group and start back to the dorms. They've heard enough of what I imagine they consider bullshit, especially the God stuff, which so many of them resent. I was the same way most of my life. Some of the other inmates, however, look genuinely moved, and Vic earns strong applause.

I always wish an addict's vow to quit is his last, and maybe it is with this guy. One thing is for certain, given all my own failed vows and promises to never drink or drug again, I'm no one to talk. But it's what he didn't say that suggests he might be up against more than he lets on. To be busted in Mexico and Canada, and only once in America, signals to me that he might be a mule, a smuggler. If he had a decent track record, junkie or not, the people he worked for will want him back, and if he was busted with a load, he owes them for the loss. And if he owes, he can't just announce he found God, get clean, and walk out of prison a free man.

After a few others share their stories, it's time to close the meeting. Sam opens a copy of the Big Book and reads The Promises.

". . . If we are painstaking about this phase of our development, we will be amazed before we are halfway through. We are going to know a new freedom and a new happiness. We will not regret the past nor . . ."

When he finishes we form a circle and join hands with the prisoners.

"God . . ." he says.

They join in, reciting in chorus.

". . . Grant me the serenity to accept the things I cannot change, the courage to change the things I can . . ."

I close my eyes. I don't suppose that most here believe. Not in God. Certainly not in Alcoholics Anonymous. They think we're some kind of cult and maybe they're right. That's where I started, too, going through the motions, not believing in anybody or anything, but then something happened. It turned into something else, and when the prayer ends, I open my eyes.

The floodlights come on, bathing the yard in bright white

light. It's a signal for the prisoners to return to the dormitories. As they trail off, one man lingers until the others are gone, so he can be alone with Sam. I don't recall seeing him in the crowd, he's just another face among many, and I only catch the end of their conversation. I'm busy putting our books and pamphlets back into the boxes we brought them in.

"You don't have to believe in anything right now," Sam says. "Just keep dreaming."

"About what?"

"A better life." He nods at the dormitories. "You don't have to live like this."

The floodlights flash off, then on again, and the young man hurries to join the others who are waiting in line to go back inside. The guards will probably bark at him for not returning right away. They'll probably give him a warning, maybe even write him up if he gets mouthy, but maybe it's worth it. That he felt the need to linger and talk with Sam. It's a good sign.

One by one the men disappear inside, until it's Sam and I, alone in the yard.

I look away.

I look beyond the dormitories. I look beyond my own expectations for why I'm here. I look beyond myself and the flood lamps and this prison and its fences topped with barbed wire into the vastness of the desert surrounding us, fading into the darkening sky.

The Last House
on the Block

Day One

Maybe your wife leaves you. Maybe it's your husband. Maybe it's another DUI. Or maybe it's no more dramatic than just waking up one morning, looking in the mirror at the puffy, bloated face you barely recognize as your own, and saying enough is enough. Today you will not drink. Today you will not put anything into your body other than coffee and food, though even the idea of food, at this particular moment, makes you queasy. Whatever your reasons, and there are many, you have finally decided to once and for all get and stay sober. This could be the beginning of a new life, and the thought of it both frightens and excites you. You are resolved. You are determined. By four o'clock that afternoon, however, about an hour or so before you normally take your first of a dozen or more drinks, your hands begin to tremble. You rub them together. Shaky hands are not that big of a deal. So far, so good, you think. But soon you're feeling nauseous, and when you look in the mirror again you see that your puffy, bloated face is bright red. Your heart is beating fast. You know that your blood pressure is rising and it scares you. Maybe going cold turkey isn't the smartest idea. Maybe you should start this sobriety thing with just two or three drinks the first day, then one or two the next, tapering down over several days instead of total abstinence right off the bat. Then you remember that you've tried this approach before. Actually you've tried this approach quite a few times before and inside of a week you've always conveniently forgotten about trying altogether.

No.

You have to tough it out. So you do this time what you've been told to do in the past but never did. You go to one of those stupid meetings and sit there, clutching the arms of the chair, listening to a bunch of idiots talk about how grateful they are not to have to pick up a drink today. To make matters worse, you've begun sweating heavily, and your heart again, it's beating even faster. You have every intention of ditching at the break and making a beeline to the liquor store, and you would have, if not for some do-gooder, this gray-haired, raggedy old man who is also apparently a mind reader.

"Don't split at the break. You're in the right place," he says. "It's one day at a time. And you're what, about halfway there? Here. You smoke?" He offers you a cigarette. You take it. "Let's go outside and talk."

You don't remember what he says, because your nerves are shot, your ears have started ringing, and all you can think about is a drink, but when they call everyone in for the second half of the meeting, you follow the guy back inside. How a stranger can have any influence over you, you have no idea, and for no reason other than that you showed up for the meeting, you're given a cheap little plastic thing, about the size of a poker chip. On one side it says *Keep Coming Back*. On the other it says *Welcome*. The old man tells you it's called a Surrender Chip and then he scribbles something on a piece of paper and stuffs it into your shirt pocket. He says to call him before you pick up a drink. Sure, you think. Why would you call someone when you *want* to drink, so you can be told *not* to drink? It doesn't make sense.

Nonetheless, you head straight home that night rather than stopping off at a bar or liquor store. Instead you plan to go right to bed, and you do. But sleep? No way. You're used to drinking yourself into unconsciousness, and now, without the booze to knock you out, all you can do is lie there, staring at the ceiling, perspiring and shaking. You're running a fever, too. You know this without taking your temperature because your face is burning and your head is pounding. It's like the flu, a really bad case of it.

You hear a sparrow chirp.

Then you hear several sparrows chirping. You switch on the light. There are no sparrows. You wonder, as you turn off the light and lie back down on the bed, if you should've checked yourself into a hospital instead of riding this out solo. There are medications for these things, so you don't hallucinate, have a seizure, or stroke out because your blood pressure spikes off the charts. They also have nurse's aides who regularly change the bedding, which you could use about now. The sheets are soaked through to the mattress, and your stomach, well, it's not doing so great, either. Something foul and hot is on its way up. You bolt for the bathroom. The poor nurse's aides would help with this mess, too, but here you are. Alone. Even bent over the toilet, you are thinking of one thing. A drink. One good slug of vodka would make all this go away.

Day Eight

You still sweat profusely. Your hands still shake. Your heart still beats fast. Your head still pounds and no amount of Aleve, Tylenol, or old-fashioned aspirin does the least bit of good. As for the nausea, it hasn't gone away, either. You have also developed the runs. Oddly, for some reason unbeknownst to you, the idea of attending a meeting crosses your mind, but there's no way you can leave the house. You can't even make it into work and have to call in sick. Your nerves are shot, and when you collapse on the couch, after staggering out of the bathroom, it feels like an electrical current is shooting up your spine. Your entire body is a live wire, buzzing all over, from head to foot.

All you want to do is sleep, except you can't, and when out of utter exhaustion you do drowse off, you're abruptly awakened by nightmares, bathed in more sweat. Again you think about a drink. Just one and your pain and agony would be nothing more than a memory. Your body is craving it. Your mind is demanding it. Fix me, it says. Help me help you. But when you stand, you're light-headed, you grow dizzy and have to sit back down. All this sweating, all these trips to the bathroom, means your body is cleansing itself of the toxins you've dumped into it.

One moment you want to cry.

The next you want to scream. A second later you're enraged and want to slam your fist through the wall. Then suddenly you're fatigued and depressed and want to curl up in a ball and die. Your skin is itchy, like insects are crawling all over you. Mostly they're on your legs and you scratch and scratch your calves and shins until they're slick with blood. There's nothing left in your stomach and hasn't been for days because the very thought of food sickens you, so now you have the dry heaves. Yet again you think of a drink and how it would instantly make you better.

How did you get to this point? When did the booze turn on you?

You drank, in part, to avoid feeling whatever troubled you. You drank to avoid suffering. Now, in getting sober, it's as if you're dying *not* to suffer.

You're finally ready to give in, and maybe you would have, the same as all the other times you tried to quit and failed, but two things change in or around the sixth day. You don't recall exactly because your brain is foggy, and you've been slipping in and out of consciousness. So far as you remember, though, the first change is that you're so dehydrated that you crave water instead of booze and find yourself drinking tons of it. And you're able to hold it down. The second is, when you glimpse yourself in the dresser mirror, you notice that your face isn't so puffy and bloated. The redness has faded, too, and your eyes, they're not bloodshot anymore. You like it. How you look. Although you still feel terrible, and your throat is raw from all the retching, just that one glimpse in the mirror reminds you of what it's like to be healthy, and, in reminding you, actually makes you *feel* a little healthier. And in this case a little means a lot.

By the eighth day, the severity of your withdrawal symptoms begins to subside. It happens slowly, yes, but you are thankful for any improvement, however small. You are proud of yourself for weathering what you believe to be the worst of the storm, and you attribute your success to your incredible strength, determination, and perseverance. In fact, you're feeling good enough to hop in the shower, put on some nice clean clothes, and maybe go to another one of those stupid meetings.

If that raggedy old drunk you met is at the meeting tonight, he'll be impressed to see that you're looking better. Of course you don't care one way or the other what he thinks.

You're fine now.

You don't need his or anyone's help. That you've proven. The only reason you're going to a meeting is because there's nothing else to do, you're bored and want to get out of the house. Don't read any more into it.

Day Thirty

You are wrong about weathering the worst of the storm. The physical withdrawals are horrible, no doubt about it, but you soon realize that the hardest part has just begun. The real war is fought on the constantly shifting battlefield of the mind. Invisible snipers are lying in wait, and the second you think you're safe is the second you walk into their crosshairs. IEDs are buried just beneath the surface of this road you travel, and if you get lazy or complacent, if you don't carefully watch your every step, it'll be the last one you take before you pick up a drink.

The voice in your head that tells you it's okay to have a drink gets louder as you navigate the minefield of your first thirty days of sobriety. But make no mistake. You're still deep in country. You're still under heavy fire, and the battlefield is strewn with bodies of those who never saw it coming, who didn't take cover, who didn't have a plan. That voice is the voice of the enemy, and because it speaks your language, because it tells you what you want to hear, you might believe that you're in the clear.

You do, after all, *look* better. You do, after all, *feel* better. This A.A. nonsense about your never being able to drink again is just that, nonsense, and when you return to work, and everyone wants to go for a drink after they clock out, you're torn. Why can't you go? One of the biggest drawbacks of not drinking is the misconception that you'll never have fun again. What's a party without booze? What's going out on the town if you can't have a few? Or even sex? You've had some good times in the sack when you were drunk. Then again, when you were drunk, there were also times when you couldn't get it up. But you don't think about that. It's called euphoric recall where all you remember is how good alcohol made you feel and how it will make you feel good again. That's where the other voice checks the first. This one says that you don't have a good time when you drink. You get loud and obnoxious and say and do things that you have to apologize for the next day. You also end up drinking alone because the people you went out with go home after two or three while you're just getting started. And getting started carries over to the next day, the one after that, and so on and so forth. Your personal party has no end.

It kills you to pass on the invitation, but, damn it, you do. You guess it's because you made a crazy promise to yourself not to drink, though honestly, in the back of your mind, you know it's about much more. A bona fide crisis of conscience. The raggedy old man's voice echoes in your head: "One drink is too many and a hundred is never enough," or what about that other cliché of how A.A. ruins your drinking, suggesting that if you were to take a drink it would come with a healthy dose of guilt and regret? If the withdrawals weren't so recent, it might be easier to forget what you had to go through to get this far, all that sweating, the shakes, nausea and accompanying headaches, fever, and auditory hallucinations.

So, damn it again, instead of indulging with your coworkers, you drag yourself to another one of those stupid meetings.

Strangely, when it's over, the desire to drink has disappeared, and on the advice of the old man, who turns out to be a former career marine who retired at the rank of sergeant major, you go to the early bird meeting the next morning before work. By the end of your first thirty days, you've attended something like thirty meetings. Also, where before you hesitate labeling yourself an alcoholic when the secretary of the meeting tells everyone to introduce themselves by their first name and the disease from which they suffer, you give in and say it. Despite all you've been through, you still think of alcoholics as those pitiful souls passed out on the sidewalks and alleys of skid row, not someone like yourself who holds a job, has a roof over his head, and drives a fairly new car. Supposedly this declaration is the first big hurdle you have to overcome, admitting you're a drunk, admitting you have a problem, because you can't begin to fix something if you don't believe it's broken. By no stretch of the imagination does this imply that you don't still have your reservations about A.A., especially the Higher Power stuff. Like it or not, however, you do have to agree that a lot of the stories you hear from the others about their drinking reminds you of your own. At the very least, whether you embrace the label of alcoholic or not, you find comfort in knowing that you're not the only messed-up person around here.

They have another chip for drunks who make it thirty days without a drink. It's a cheap little thing, this one made of aluminum instead of plastic, stamped with the A.A. circle and triangle symbol on one side, and the Serenity Prayer on the other. You don't want to stand up and take one when your time comes, because you don't want the attention of everyone clapping and shouting out "How did you do it?" but the old Sergeant Major says you have to.

He says it's not really about you, anyway.

Rather it's to show that if a wretched drunk such as yourself can survive a whole month without a drink, then there's hope for those in the room with less time than you. Your misery, grief, and despair somehow become a shining example for the grief, misery, and despair of others about to embark on perhaps the hardest but most important journey of their lives.

Day Sixty

You almost don't make this next stretch. You find that your brain remains foggy. That you forget the simplest things. You're at home, for instance, and you're looking for a pair of scissors, but by the time you go from the bedroom to the junk drawer in the kitchen you don't remember what you're looking for. Once, while stopped in your car at a red light, you react as if the light has turned green when it hasn't and you step on the gas, nearly causing a wreck.

Another time, around the ordinary drinking hour, your nerves are so frazzled that you can't catch your breath. You think you're having an asthma attack, only you don't have asthma, and as far as irritability goes, on a scale of one to ten, you're at an eight or nine on a daily basis. Withdrawals also affect your mental faculties, clarity of mind, and memory, and though their severity varies from drunk to drunk, yours seem to have gotten worse instead of better in the weeks after you took your last drink.

The battle of the mind is still alive and well, and you wonder if there isn't some kind of middle ground where you can drink a little now and then without going overboard. It could be bunk, this A.A. belief that once you've crossed the line into alcoholism you can never safely drink again. Maybe you could sign up for some kind of professional, science-based program that teaches you how to control and enjoy your drinking like a normal person.

You research it.

There are a few programs out there that fit the bill, but they're not cheap, and their claims that they can train you to drink in moderation, when you look closely at them, seem dubious at best. For that matter, none of these alcohol and drug programs are cheap. Far from it. It's a booming industry in a booming market with an endless supply of alcoholics and addicts moving through the revolving doors of recovery homes across the globe. And you're sure that all too often the bottom line for these businesses, and they are businesses, is more about the almighty dollar than sobriety.

You've lived long enough to become a cynic.

Much as you have issues with A.A., it doesn't cost you a cent, though they do pass the hat around at the end of the meetings, asking for a buck or two. That's hardly a hustle, and for those most down on their luck, no one blinks an eye if they can't contribute. It is, for many, what A.A. refers to as the last house on the block. And it's here, when you get out of one of those expensive rehabs, that your counselors will tell you to go, anyway, slipping you a Big Book on your way out the door. Maybe it's just as well that you start at the last house on the block and save the state or your insurance company tens of thousands of dollars. But do you actually have to move into this house? Do you have to live in A.A. forever? The more you question, the more the bright idea of a drink pops into your head until one night, on your way home from work, your car automatically steers itself into the parking lot of a liquor store.

You kill the engine. You reach for the door handle. You open it. You get out of your car. You tell yourself you're only going in for a pack of smokes, but you know that's a lie. Is it coincidence that you left your cell phone at work, so you couldn't call that old marine before you buy a bottle, or did your subconscious play a role in it? Are you setting yourself up? Did the setup begin well before your car went on autopilot and steered itself into the lot? Probably. But you're not one for psychoanalyzing your every thought or action. Either way, there's one of those ancient pay phones right next to the front door of the liquor store, and try as you might, you can't pretend that you don't see it without this flood of guilt sweeping over you. Just as the car steered itself, a similar force takes control of you, and against your will and desire to drink, and that desire is *strong*, you pick up the receiver and drop some coins into the slot. Your next hope, as you dial his number and listen to it ring, is that he won't pick up. This way you can tell yourself that you tried, you gave it your best shot, but oh well, he wasn't there, so you can hang up and go for the kill without further delay. But, damn it yet again, he picks up, and since he's a mind reader, he knows immediately why you're calling. You expect him to give you a lecture, but instead he tells you some lousy joke he just heard, a joke that has nothing to do with drinking, and there you are, outside of a liquor store on an ancient pay phone, laughing. Only you're not laughing at the joke. You're laughing at yourself, because you're relieved, just hearing the old man's voice. The desire to drink somehow vanishes and you haven't said a word about alcohol.

You don't have to tell him where you are. You don't have to tell him how close you are to falling off the wagon. He knows intuitively. He knows because this is the first time you've called him, so all he tells you, after you shoot the breeze for a while, and before you hang up, is that you did the right thing by calling him. Some days are rougher than others and we wonder what the point of it all is. What does it matter if we live or die sober? Except it does matter, he says.

Because *you* matter.

You fill in the blanks yourself. It's about self-respect. It's about self-worth. It's about whether you want to stumble through this imperfect world in a drunken stupor, whining and crying about life's injustices, or embrace what's left of it sober and clearheaded. The great thing, as you approach sixty days, is that you've begun to see drinking as something over which you now have the power of choice. In the not-so-distant past, when every cell in your body was screaming for a drink, it was the other way around. Booze had you by the jugular and wouldn't let go.

You get back into your car and drive away.

The next day, inspired by your newfound resolve, you go through the contact list on your smartphone and choose whose numbers to keep and whose to delete. It is one of your hardest duties to date but you convince yourself that it's necessary. That it's for your own good. Your own safety. Who, honestly, are your real friends anyway? Who, honestly, are friends only because you drank and used together? And who, though still drinkers, will not put your sobriety at risk? This last group must be considered the most carefully. Just because you have a problem with alcohol doesn't mean your friends who still partake do. Do you, in the name of self-preservation, delete them from the list, too? If so, that pretty much eliminates everybody you know outside of A.A. You decide to keep those in the gray area, so long as they're okay with not drinking in front of you, and that includes even a glass of wine if you decide to go out for dinner together.

The process of revising your contact list is the process of examining past and present relationships, and, by extension, the process of revising yourself. Scratching out the names and numbers of those long considered friends strikes you as heartless and cruel. Maybe, when you feel more secure about your sobriety, you can open the door a little wider, but for the foreseeable future you think it wise to err on the side of caution. Sobriety can be a lonely journey, with so much of the fight occurring inside your own head, but if it's any consolation, you are starting to think of a couple of people in A.A. as friends. This comes as a surprise to you, since you generally have a low regard for the entire human race.

For the next week you're on what is known in A.A. as *a pink cloud*. Life is good. You haven't been clean and sober sixty days since you started drinking in your teens and you're middle-aged now.

As for taking your two-month chip, which is again another cheap little aluminum thing, you're no more comfortable standing up and having everyone clap and shout "How did you do it?" than you were thirty days ago. But, as before, the Sergeant Major reminds you that it's not about you. If a seemingly hopeless drunk such as yourself can survive two treacherous months without a drop of booze, then you are a shining example for others beginning perhaps the hardest, most important journey of their lives.

Day Ninety to Six Months

You'd like to think, after six months without a drink, that you would be able to sleep through the night. One lousy night. But you would be wrong. The insomnia persists, and you're still dragging yourself out of bed, tired and worn out before the day has even begun. At meetings, when you're called on to introduce yourself and state the nature of your disease, you give your first name followed by the label *insomniac alcoholic* rather than just *alcoholic*. You think you're being funny but no one laughs. Insomnia is so common in early recovery that at best most find your attempt at humor sadly unoriginal. You soon go back to the simple truth that you're a plain old alcoholic, no cute embellishments, adjectives, or adverbs attached.

Along with the sleeplessness, everything else is basically the same. You still think about a drink, if not every day, then every other. Your brain is still foggy, too, and you forget random words.

Your mind drifts, so that when someone asks you something, and you're supposed to respond, you have no idea what they said. This generates many strange, awkward looks, particularly from those who don't know you. Those who do, and who know what you're battling, feel bad for you. It's probably harder on them to see you struggle to get out a sentence than it is for you to stutter and stammer your way through it.

The former marine assures you that your mental confusion is part and parcel to recovery, as is your insomnia. The brain, he says, is misfiring. The brain is short-circuiting because it's in the process of rewiring itself after years of alcohol abuse. The lights will flicker and flash and sometimes they'll burn out all at once, leaving you in complete darkness. But he tells you not to worry. Eventually everything comes back on and burns brighter than ever. And eventually you'll sleep through the night. You ask how long *eventually* is, and he shrugs. It might clear up tomorrow. It might take another few months. He's heard of insomnia and mental confusion lasting up to a year or more, and in some cases, such as *wet brain*, the damage is permanent. That scares you and the old guy sees it on your face. He smiles. Don't worry, he says, if you had wet brain you'd lurch to one side when you walk, and you don't lurch.

This much is true. For some reason, though, it doesn't make you feel better, and unfortunately your memory loss is not selective. There are plenty of things you still keenly *remember* about getting drunk that you would rather forget but cannot. The nasty hangovers, for one. The pounding headaches and nausea. Most of all you don't miss waking up, or rather *coming to* and not remembering what you did the night before, and then panicking, bolting upright in bed and running out of the house to inspect your car for damages, or, God forbid, blood on the front grill. How could you forgive yourself if you killed some innocent soul driving home in a blackout?

On a less serious note, without all the empty calories from the booze, you're losing that roll around your belly. Let's not get carried away, you tell yourself, but is it also possible that the crow's feet around your eyes are diminishing? Alcohol ages you, wears you down, but to a small degree the process is reversible once you quit poisoning yourself. The reasons for getting sober run far deeper than wrinkles and visceral fat, but vanity is nonetheless a motivator, and you will unabashedly take your motivation where you can get it.

What does *not* motivate you, however, is the old marine's suggestion that it's time for you to get a sponsor and start working the Twelve Steps. You're good with the First Step in that you're finally able to admit you're a real, dyed-in-the-wool alcoholic and that your life has become unmanageable, but that Second Step about believing in a Power greater than yourself still bugs you. The word *power* is a euphemism, so that they can ease nonbelievers like yourself into the idea of God, because the Third Step comes right out with it, again with some wiggle room, using the caveat of this God being one of your *own understanding*. This means that if you have problems with regular old religion gods, you should feel free to make up your own. The kicker is, where the first couple of Steps focus on reflection and introspection, the Third requires action, demanding that you turn your will and your life over to the care of this God, whatever it may be. The Steps only get harder from there with the next ones basically asking you to acknowledge your screwups, confess them to someone you trust not to spread your darkest secrets all over town, ask your God to help you not screw up in the future, and more or less apologize to all the people you screwed over. If you can further redress whatever emotional or material damage you caused them, great, but if that simply isn't possible, you need at the very least to accept responsibility for your actions. If nothing else, this will hopefully help you clear your conscience, and a clear conscience, so you're told, goes a long way in keeping a drunk sober.

There are exceptions where admitting your wrongdoing to the injured party might backfire and do more harm than good, such as telling your wife about all the affairs you had while you were drinking. In cases such as these, along with capital crimes that have no statute of limitations, it may be best to keep your mouth shut and make a sincere, personal vow to never do these bad things again. In return for completing all Twelve Steps, you're supposed to be relieved of the obsession to drink, and after that you're supposed to have some sort of spiritual awakening and pass on what you've learned to other drunks. This is a gross oversimplification of the A.A. program, but it's basically the gist of it.

And it requires a lot of work.

It requires a lot of soul-searching, and when you tell the Sergeant Major that you just don't feel ready yet to get a sponsor and do all this stuff, you expect an argument. You expect him to try to convince you otherwise, but he only shrugs as if to say, okay, fine, have it your way. We all go at our own pace. Coming from a former marine trained in barking orders, you are relieved and impressed.

Tonight he is secretary of the meeting. He calls on you to

take your six-month chip, which is another cheap little aluminum thing, and as usual you are no more comfortable standing up and having everyone clap and shout "How did you do it?" than you were before. But at least it's settling in, without your having to be told that this ceremony has little to do with you. Instead, if a seemingly hopeless drunk such as yourself can survive six long months without a drink or a drug then you are a shining example for the newcomers in the room just beginning perhaps the hardest, most important journey of their lives.

Nine Months to a Year

You are amazed.

You are surprised. Most of all you are proud of yourself for not taking a drink for 365 consecutive days. When you first came into this room, had someone said that you'd make it this far, you would've thought that they were crazy or stupid or both. But here you are, a year later, feeling healthy and strong and alive again in ways you never imagined possible. That doesn't mean you can relax, though. That doesn't mean you can rest on your laurels, get cocky, and let your guard down. You still can't go near a bar. You still can't eat at a restaurant that has a bar. Obviously you can't yet go to a party where people are drinking, or even push your grocery cart through the liquor aisle at the grocery store. When you watch TV, you still have to switch channels when the beer commercials come on. This means you watch a lot of different programs. If you're driving, listening to the radio and a certain song comes on, one that reminds you of your drinking and drugging days, you have to change the channel. This means you listen to a lot of new music. Returning to old haunts, which likely includes your own neighborhood, also remains a dangerous trigger. Mouthwash is off-limits, too, if it contains alcohol. The sting of it on your tongue, the taste, the mere *smell* of alcohol can set off a craving. In the first year of sobriety, you can't do much of anything except attend meetings and do your best to avoid places, persons, and things that might weaken your resolve to not drink.

In the early months, when meetings ended, you always used to hurry straight for the door. Now you find yourself hanging around afterward and helping clean up, maybe wash out the coffeepots, or restack the chairs. Sometimes you'll share a smoke with the Sergeant Major after the meeting lets out. And a lot of these people who you thought were losers aren't really losers at all. Most, it seems, are here to help keep each other from getting drunk. The more you get to know them, the less you judge them, but you're also no fool.

You're aware of what's happening.

You're aware that the repetitive act of reading the A.A. Preamble, the Twelve Steps and Twelve Traditions, and a portion of Chapter Five from the Big Book at the start of each and every meeting is a common indoctrination technique. Reciting the same words and concepts over and over drives the principles of the program deep into your mind, as does having to state your name and the nature of your disease each time you introduce yourself and then again every time before you address the group. The goal is to infiltrate the subconscious. The goal is to brainwash, to convert, and you're reminded of this old movie called *Invasion of the Body Snatchers* where these extraterrestrial parasites get inside of you and take over your mind and body, destroying your ability to think and reason. Once the process is complete, your old self disintegrates into dust and you're transformed into one of the Pod People. The next thing you know you'll be like those Jehovah Witnesses going door-to-door, except instead of peddling the word of God you'll be preaching the wonders and miracles of sobriety.

Do you want to be like that?

Your head full of clichés and recitations? A walking talking zombie for the cult of A.A.? You know they're pulling at you, and if you don't break free, and do it soon, you're going down, never to return, certainly not the same person anyway. It's almost as if you're at a crossroads and don't know which way to turn. There's still that voice inside you that says you made it this far all on your own incredible strength, determination, and perseverance. But then the other voice pipes up, saying sure, you're entitled to take some credit, but don't kid yourself, you couldn't have done it alone. This voice also tells you that maybe it's time to quit screwing around, ask the old Sergeant to be your sponsor, and get to work on the Steps. Think of it as an insurance policy. If disaster strikes, and it will, for at some point or another life has a way of tearing down what we build, you want full coverage against drinking because of it.

The first-year chip is not a cheap little aluminum thing. This one is made of bronze, and you like how it feels in your hand, the heft of it, real metal, thick and strong. As the group is shouting "How did you do it?" you notice a middle-aged guy sitting alone, far in the back. You've never seen him before, and he's sweating, clutching the arms of his chair, same as you the first time you took a seat in this room one year ago today. No way, you think, is this sorry bastard going to make it, and you figure that the last thing he wants to hear is a bunch of idiots, one of whom would be you, talk about how grateful they are not to have to pick up a drink today. If not for some do-gooder, he would've left at the break and made a beeline straight to the nearest liquor store. But this do-gooder, who also happens to be a mind reader now, offers him a cigarette while another do-gooder, a gray-haired, raggedy old man, looks on from nearby, shaking his head and smiling.

Damn it, you say, but not out loud. The words are in your mind. Why should you care about somebody you've never met before? Why would you scribble your number on a piece of paper and stuff it into his shirt pocket, telling him to give you a call before he picks up a drink?

You didn't see it coming.

You didn't know you had it in you to care about a complete stranger. And as far as that chip in his hand goes, the cheapest of the cheap plastic ones they give you on your first day, you finally realize it's just as important as the bronze one you're holding.

If you can survive the next twenty-four hours without a drink, then maybe it's time to give back what was so freely given to you and help another drunk begin perhaps the hardest, most important journey of his life, too.

Leaving Las Vegas

as Vegas is about a three-hour drive from my house in Lake Arrowhead, and back in the day, under the influence of alcohol, coke, or meth, I could make it in just over two. Easy. But this time, when I come to Vegas, it is with my wife and youngest son. I do not speed, at least not excessively, and I am no longer drinking or using. Instead I am here to visit my middle son who works in law enforcement. He lives in Wyoming and we don't see each other nearly enough, but he's taking part in counterterrorism tactical drills on the outskirts of Vegas, and this is a good opportunity to drive out and visit with him after he finishes training. We meet up with Logan and his girlfriend for dinner at seven o'clock at Cucina by Wolfgang Puck on October 1, 2017. In three hours and five minutes, the deadliest mass shooting in U.S. history will occur.

There is a time, early in my sobriety, when I could not have gone to Vegas without putting myself in serious jeopardy of relapsing. But that time has passed. Alcohol no longer concerns me. I no longer fear being around it. When the hostess seats us, and the waiter comes by to take our drink orders, Nate leans in close to me. He lowers his voice.

"It won't bother you if I have a glass of wine?"

"No," I say. "Go right ahead."

"You sure?"

I smile.

"You're twenty-one," I say.

He's a considerate young man. All my sons are considerate and thoughtful, including Andy, my oldest, who is getting married in two weeks and could not make this trip. They have seen their father as a drunk and they have seen him as a better man. I have regained the respect I lost but only because they have allowed it, only because they have opened their hearts to me again, and keeping that respect, which is also their love, has everything to do with my sobriety.

My wife Paula, Logan, and his girlfriend also order wine. Paula rarely drinks and never when we go out for dinner alone. This is another thing I don't understand. Why bother drinking if you don't want to get drunk, really drunk? This, plainly, is another reason why she can safely drink and I cannot. Once I start, I have no cut-off point short of unconsciousness.

In my teens, alcohol made me silly and cheerful. I could count on having a good time. By my late twenties, however, my moods and behavior became increasingly less predictable, and if there is one person at the table who concerns me, it is Logan. I love all of my boys the same and differently, for they are each their own person. They each, in their own ways, embody both strengths and weaknesses of their parents, but Logan is too much like myself with his resolute temperament and tough exterior masking deep emotional vulnerabilities. I've seen him drunk before and his disposition can fluctuate widely from good-naturedness to anger without a moment's notice. This same month last year, when I visited him in Wyoming, he participated in a fundraiser for our wounded Green Berets, Army Rangers, and their Gold Star families, and after leading a tactical unit in an urban-breach exhibition, his team bought him drinks at the bar.

He seemed fine.

He seemed like a happy drunk. But later, on the drive back to our motel, his mood turned dark. I saw too much of myself in my boy that night, and it scared me. It scares me now. A single incident like this is not necessarily indicative of alcoholism, but law enforcement and military, like writers, are notorious for their drinking and partying, and so I worry. I worry that if he is not careful he will damage what he has with the pretty young girl seated beside him, this girl named Courtney who has just moved in with him, as I damaged what I had with his mother. The same is true for Paula. She's endured her fair share of misery from me, too, but I straightened up in time. I like to think that I learned. I like to think that together we saved what I could've so easily destroyed again. And I like to think that should any of my sons one day need this lesson that they learn it more thoroughly and quickly than their father.

The waiter is looking at me. I'm the last to order.

"And you?" he says.

"Diet Coke," I say.

The waiter leaves, and it crosses my mind what reaction I

would've gotten if I'd jokingly asked for a whiskey straight up. Or vodka with a twist. It wouldn't have been funny. Terrifying, maybe, but not funny.

About a mile away, as we're enjoying dinner, Stephen Paddock is locked in his suite on the thirty-second floor of the Mandalay Bay Resort and Casino. He checked in three days earlier, but he doesn't move into this particular room until the night before the attack, which, according to a hotel source, is given to him free because he was a good customer. This one has a much better view of the Las Vegas Strip and the Route 91 Harvest, a country music festival across the street, not far from where Paula, Nate, and I are staying at the Monte Carlo. Logan and his girlfriend have a room at the nearby Circus Circus.

Obviously I have no idea what Paddock is doing in the last hours leading up to the massacre, but I can imagine. I can see him setting up the shooting tripods police later find in his room. I can see him loading the high-capacity magazines on his semiautomatic rifles, several with scopes, and I can see him jotting down numbers on a piece of paper on the coffee table. Calculations of distance and trajectory from his suite to the concert site below. He thinks he is smart. That he knows firearms and how best to use them. He is, however, disappointed that he was unable to purchase tracer ammunition at a gun show some weeks earlier. These are bullets with a pyrotechnic charge that, when fired, leave an illuminated path, and they would've helped him see where his shots were going in the darkness. They would've helped him kill more.

It's unfortunate that he'll have to make do without tracers, but it's nothing more than a small setback for such a fine sharp-shooter. Such a great fucking marksman, blasting into a crowd, like shooting into a barrel of fish. He feels the time is now. He feels a sense of urgency, for he has booked rooms before in two other hotels overlooking concerts, and both times he fails to follow through with his plans. Is it because he suddenly has a change of heart? Is it because, if only for a split second, he sees himself for the sick and wicked man he is?

I doubt it.

He has a penchant for prostitutes, violent sex, and rape fantasies, and brags to the women about his ex-con father, a bank robber, and how he inherited his "bad blood." How he was "born bad." If he means *bad* as in *badass*, then he sounds like a real tough guy to me, especially the part where he ties the women up and has them "scream for help" for six thousand dollars a night.

Now I'm outside of the room. In the hallway.

Maybe I'm a guest passing by, or a maid with her cart of linens and cleaning supplies, but I see the door open just enough for Paddock to slip his hand out. I see his hand disappear, leaving the DO NOT DISTURB placard hanging from the knob. It swings gently from side to side as the door shuts and locks behind him.

I don't check the time. I'm only guessing. But it would have to be close to eight when we finish dinner and the waiter takes our plates. I make a mental note that nobody ordered a second drink, including Logan. If I were him at his ripe old age of twenty-eight, I'd have easily been on my fourth or fifth by now, making an ass of myself, and it encourages me that he's able to stop at one. Then again maybe he's holding strong because he knows I'm watching. Maybe he's planning on hitting the bar at one of the casinos and getting smashed as soon as he escapes my attention. I'm a cynic when it comes to my sons, *especially* my sons. I've read widely on the subject of addiction and can tick off all kinds of facts, particularly the one about children of drunks being four times more susceptible to alcoholism than children whose parents are not drunks. Double that figure if the child starts drinking before the age of fourteen. My boys clearly fall into the first category, and I'm pretty sure, since none of them are exactly angels, that they also meet the criteria of the second.

Dessert arrives.

I'm skipping this course but Nate wants me to share his tiramisu with him.

"I'm stuffed," I say.

"Me, too," he says. "Help me out. Don't want to waste food, right? You're the one always bitching about not wasting food."

He has me there.

"Wiseass," I say. "Give me your fork."

When they were growing up, I used to make them sit at the table until they finished their plates. I used to tell them stories about how their grandparents suffered through the Great Depression, and how, when I was a kid and my parents broke up and my mother moved me, my brother, and sister to LA, that there were a few days here and there when we didn't have food at all. I used to tell them that by the third day your stomach stops growling and the aching stops.

As I'm helping Nate with his tiramisu, Courtney catches his eye.

"So Nate," she asks, "are you still in college?"

"I didn't go to college."

Logan has a bachelor's in criminal justice. Andy, my oldest, earned an MFA in studio art and works at a gallery in Beverly Hills. Nate is the outlier, the rebel who defied his father's direct orders that he would and must attend college. His obstinance, however, wore me down, and eventually my commands turned to supplications, followed by weeks of brooding silence, and finally acceptance that this son has different plans. I'm fine with his decision now, yet when the question pops up in mixed company I still feel the need to defend what I assume others may see as my parental failure. Aren't all kids supposed to go to college, and, if not, aren't they all losers? Isn't that how college-educated people often judge those without college degrees? Courtney has a bachelor's in accounting.

"He's into computers," I say. "He's been making good money since he was a teenager."

It's true. Mid-five figures at fourteen. Enough, anyway, to live well in a nice house in San Diego since he moved out at eighteen.

"Oh," she says. "That's great."

But I'm not so sure she means it. It's the sort of response people give when they realize they've inadvertently broached a touchy subject. So it's Logan's turn to step up for his little brother.

"He runs his own cybersecurity company."

"Really?"

"It's not just me," he says. "I have a partner. We run it together."

Nate is modest, and if not for his muscular build and male-model good looks, you'd never know he's a computer geek who spends so much of his time alone in his home office that he's become a bona fide borderline social anxiety case.

"Tell her about it," I say.

"Not now."

"Come on," I say, "it's pretty interesting stuff."

I nudge him with my elbow. He nudges me back, but I get my way. He looks at Courtney.

"It's not that big a deal," he says. "We scrape the dark web and parse through the data to see if we can find any references to leaked personal information. This can be extremely important to businesses to protect their intellectual property and customer data."

"In English, please," Logan says.

Nate blinks.

"I guess you could just say we watch out for companies, and if they have an issue, we eliminate the threat before it becomes a problem."

"What sort of companies?" Courtney asks.

"That I can't talk about."

None of us press him, and it's just as well. We've finished dessert, and except for Nate, who is not the least bit interested in gambling, we're all itching now to split up and watch our money disappear into what might as well be the dark web of computerized slot machines.

Stephen Paddock is a compulsive gambler. He is also wealthy. His game of choice is video poker, and he's been known to play for ten hours at a stint, occasionally winning thousands on a single hand, but usually losing far more. The computerized games are set heavily in the house's favor, and though Paddock knows this, he prefers video poker over the real thing because of his aversion to people. The machines require no human interaction. He is sixty-four years old. His attire does not suggest a man of wealth, often going unshaven, in sweatpants and flip-flops, even while playing in Vegas's exclusive, restricted-access areas for high rollers. He is a loner. But he is a loner with a high profile among the casino bosses who reward him for his loyalty with big hotel perks. Paddock is described by personnel as quiet, perhaps stand-offish, while neighbors recall Paddock's girlfriend, Marilou Danley, as outgoing and friendly. Some say that they made a great pair. Others report frequently hearing him screaming and shouting and berating her.

An Australian acquaintance of Paddock's refers to him as highly intelligent, conservative, guarded, methodical. A strategic, planning type of guy. Paddock's brother, Eric, says his eldest sibling was like a dad to him. That he took him camping. That he was a *good guy*. But Paddock had little contact with his two other younger brothers, according to Eric, because one is a very different man and the other used to beat Stephen up when they were kids. Stephen Paddock is apparently an unforgiving, judgmental man, and yet there seems to be no ideological motivations for his heinous slaughter of innocent children, women, and men.

In Stephen Paddock's case, I am unforgiving as well. May the bastard burn in hell.

At the time of the shooting I am playing Paddock's favorite game at the Aria Resort and Casino. I am sitting at the bar, drinking a Coke, and actually winning on the video poker machine in front of me. Every now and then I take a break and look up at the flat-screens mounted above the bar. A football game is underway. The people around me are excited, shouting and rooting for their preferred players, their preferred teams. But I'm not interested in the game. I don't follow football or any other sports except boxing and college wrestling. Still, I like to see people enjoy themselves, and so their boisterousness doesn't bother me. All the bottles lined up in neat rows behind the counter don't bother me, either. Lights shine upward from underneath the glass shelves that hold the bottles, so that the liquor inside them glows, soft amber for the whiskey and brandy, translucent crystal for the vodka and gin. Set against a backdrop of mirrors, they make an appealing presentation, and I admit that my eyes linger on the glimmering, cobalt blue bottle of Skyy. How often did I start a binge with the more expensive vodkas and end it with cheap stuff? How can the contents of these pretty bottles be so lethal to one and so harmless and pleasurable to another?

Purportedly Stephen Paddock regularly drank a constant stream of booze while he sat and played the same kind of game I'm playing now. For all I know, I could be sitting on the same stool he once sat on. He was, like myself, an alcoholic, and news reports will later suggest that his drinking contributed to his mental deterioration. Mental illness and alcoholism, however, cannot and never will, in any conceivable way, explain an act that can only be defined as evil.

I press a button.

The cards on the screen line up, four of a kind, all deuces, and the next thing I know I'm 250 dollars richer.

I've been at it a while, a couple hours it seems, trying to kill time while Paula plays the slots. But for once I'd like to quit while

I'm ahead, and I'm about to call Paula, tell her come on, let's get out of here, when a middle-aged man rushes up to the bar. One sleeve of his dress coat is torn at the shoulder, the corner of his lip is split and bleeding, and the side of his face is also scratched and bleeding, as if he's been dragged across pavement or concrete. He waves to the bartender, who hurries over. The middle-aged man is Asian and speaks in broken English.

"Call the police," he says. "Please. Four Hispanic men beat and robbed me."

"In the casino?"

"In the parking lot. Hurry. They tried to steal my car. I don't let them."

Just then my cell vibrates. I look at the screen. It's a text from Logan: *Active shooter on the Strip. We're in our room. Where are you and Paula? Where is Nate? He's not answering his cell. He's not answering my texts.*

Initial reports state that Jesus Campos, an unarmed security guard, approaches Room 135 on the thirty-second floor of the Mandalay Bay Resort and Casino at 9:59 p.m. He is there to check on an open door near Paddock's suite, whereupon, after hearing "drilling sounds," he is shot through the door. About two hundred rounds are fired, one striking Campos in the leg. It is later learned that Paddock mounted security cameras in the hallway, alerting him to Campos's arrival, shooting him several minutes before opening fire from the smashed-out windows of his suite. After pressure from Mandalay Bay owners, however, police amend the timeline, contending Campos arrives on the thirty-second floor at 9:59 p.m.

but isn't shot until closer to 10:05 p.m., about the time Paddock
guns down concertgoers at a distance of approximately four hundred yards. The revised timeline could mean the difference between millions and tens of millions in payouts for the hotel's legal
defense team. Responsibility, as it translates to dollars, will likely
be measured in seconds.

In Paddock's possession are twenty-three weapons, including semiautomatic rifles replete with bump stocks that allow for
more rapid fire, scopes, and no less than two thousand rounds of
ammunition in .308 and .223 caliber. The .223 is nearly identical
to the standard cartridge of our U.S. military while the .308 is
typically associated with big game hunting.

I visualize him using multiple rifles.

I see him firing on the crowd through one window. Then I see
him running down the hall of his suite to the second window and
firing from there. He does not bother switching out magazines,
though it would only take a couple of seconds. With so many
rifles at his disposal, I suppose it might be quicker to drop an
empty gun and grab a loaded one. But I'm not sure. I'm not sure
about anything with this man who must hear the screams and
cries of the dying and wounded every time he lets up on the trigger and the blasting momentarily stops. But how could he have
ever pulled it? How could he continue to pull it, again and again,
fully aware of the carnage he's inflicting? The people are fenced in
and have nowhere to go.

The news has not yet spread. People remain transfixed in front of
slot machines, pulling levers and pushing buttons. Crowds still

surround the tables, playing poker, craps, and roulette. It's noisy with bells and whistles and laughter and shouting and the cocktail waitresses continue to serve drinks. Nothing seems out of the ordinary on this busy Sunday night at the Aria Resort and Casino.

I call Paula.

"We have to leave," I say.

"What's the matter?"

"There's a shooter on the Strip."

"What?"

"Just meet me at the escalators," I say. "We have to get back to our room."

I don't tell her about the poor guy who got beat up and robbed, but that's another reason I want to get out of here. Those lowlifes, or more like them, could be roaming the streets, looking for their next mark.

I text Logan after we hang up, telling him where we're at and that we're leaving for our hotel. The bartender is on the phone, his back to me, so I inform the guy seated next to me about the shooter.

"Oh yeah?" he says, as if it's no big deal. "I hope they get him."

Then he takes a drag off his cigarette and returns to his game.

On my way to the escalators, Logan texts me again. *I'm on the police band but it's a mess. They don't know shit. Possible 3 or 4 shooters. Mandalay Bay. Tropicana. Possible car bomb outside the Luxor.*

"Fuck," I say, under my breath.

I text Nate.

Where are you?

What if after dinner, since he doesn't gamble, he decided to sightsee the Strip and got caught in a hail of gunfire?

Paula sees me as I near the escalators.

"What's going on?"

I tell her what Logan texted me. Her eyes grow wide.

"Shit," she says. "It has to be terrorists."

Like me, she is also jumping to conclusions. I take her hand and we head for the escalators.

First we feel only the slightest rumbling, like a small, hardly measurable tremor beneath our feet. But the tremor quickly grows stronger, and it's no earthquake. Our plan is to go down the escalator or the adjoining stairway to reach the lobby, and from there ultimately the exit, but others have exactly the opposite idea, which is to say a flood of people come rushing toward us, screaming "active shooter ... active shooter," giving Paula and me a split second to make one of two choices. Either get trampled by the frenzied crowd or turn around and run with them. We choose the latter.

Country western music star Jason Aldean goes on stage at 9:40 p.m. and plays for about twenty-five minutes before Paddock sprays bullets on the crowd of twenty-two thousand people below him. He releases a dozen or more volleys in the next ten minutes, the firing ceasing at approximately 10:15 p.m. There are conflicting accounts, however, that the Las Vegas SWAT team, apparently acting on faulty information, first raided the Tropicana before they realized their monumental mistake and went to the Mandalay Bay. And even then, fearing Paddock had rigged his door with explosives, they failed to enter the suite until seventy minutes later.

It's reported that since the shooting had stopped by then, police felt no urgency to breach the room, and the first officers to arrive at the scene at 10:17 p.m. spent much of their time searching the floor's other rooms and evacuating guests. It is not reported how the responding officers and SWAT team should have reacted had the shooting resumed and more lives were lost as a result of their inaction. Some believe the risk of further deaths from Paddock opening fire again merited a more aggressive response. The Las Vegas PD defends its decision not to immediately neutralize the threat and instead wager on the odds of silence, indicating that the massacre had stopped, as opposed to the possibility that Stephen Paddock had simply paused to reload. This is not a bet I would expect law enforcement to make.

When SWAT finally breaks into the room, they find Paddock dead, apparently from a self-inflicted gunshot. I imagine he shoots himself in the head, but as of this writing, even that small detail is left unanswered in the briefings and news sources I research on the internet.

We know so little.

On the one hand, it's reported that he had no political or religious affiliations, and on the other, ISIS's official news agency, Amaq, claims Paddock was a "soldier of the Islamic State," contending that he converted to Islam several months before his explosion of terror. Amaq has been wrong in the past, but rarely, and it seems odd that in the years leading up to the massacre that Paddock took at least twenty cruises across the globe, including visits to Dubai and Abu Dhabi, Oman, the Jordanian port of Aqaba, Bahrain, and Qatar. All of these countries are on heightened alert for terrorist attacks. The FBI, however, is quick to conclude that Stephen Paddock has no connections to international or national terrorist organizations.

Fear is contagious. It envelops Paula and me and draws us into the stampede of people running up from the escalators and down across the game floor of the Aria Resort and Casino. Most of the gamblers at the slots and tables don't seem to care, hardly glancing at the rushing crowd, but there are some who join us, the looks on their faces quickly changing from startlement to horror. I question my own fear. What do those at the front of this charge know that I don't? Have they seen the shooter? Or shooters? Heard the shots or been shot at? Has a bomb gone off? Or are we caught up in the sort of mass hysteria akin to someone falsely shouting *fire* in a packed theater? If I were by myself, maybe I would've broken from the herd, reassessed, but I am with my wife and can't afford to take any chances. She is scared, and so the thing to do is separate ourselves from the fleeing crowd and the packed casino floor. If I were a terrorist, I would fire into the largest groupings possible rather than waste time moving from floor to floor, stalking individual prey. "We have to go up," I say. "Away from the crowd." We spot the hotel elevators and run to them, but there are a half dozen security guards protecting the area, only allowing entrance to those with room keys.

Paula and I rush off.

Another couple is right behind us, and when Paula and I leave, they follow. The man speaks to the woman in a foreign tongue that I don't recognize. Russian? An Eastern European language? I wonder if they think that because we're Americans we know what we're doing when really we're as frantic and confused as they are.

Paula spots a staircase.

"There," she says, pointing.

It's cordoned off with brass looper tubes. But no one is guarding it, so we squeeze by and rush up the stairs. The couple tails us. At the top we find ourselves surrounded by restaurants and shops. All of them are closed. At first glance the hallways look empty but there are others, maybe a dozen, hiding behind pillars, crouching behind concrete planters, or huddling in the alcoves of the different stores. The shops and restaurants are dark inside. Elevator music, the *Pink Panther* theme, plays over hidden speakers. A security guard runs past us. Paula shouts to him.

"What's going on?"

"I don't know," he says, and keeps running.

"Are we safe here?"

But he's gone by then, disappearing around the corner. Paula glares at me.

"Great security, huh? If he doesn't know what's happening, who the hell does?"

The couple that followed us are now at our side. They are not, as I initially thought, Eastern European, but rather Middle Eastern. I place the man in his late twenties. The woman is about the same age. She looks up from her phone and speaks with the slight hint of an Arabic accent, telling us that it's ISIS, all right, at least according to the breaking news.

"*Daesh*," the young man says. "Pigs."

He looks down at the floor, closes his eyes, and shakes his

head. After a moment he looks back up at me and holds his hand out.

"I'm sorry, my manners. I'm Omar. This is my girlfriend, Jenny."

We all shake hands and introduce ourselves and then agree that we shouldn't stand there in the hallway like sitting ducks. Omar suggests we hide in a nearby stairwell until I tell him about Logan, his tactical training, and show him his most recent text. *One shooter down at Mandalay Bay. Stay off casino floor. Safest at higher ground but stairwells are a trap.* The next best bet, we decide, is The Roasted Bean. It's like a Starbucks and it's only one shop down the way. We hide there behind the counter with another couple from Australia who had the same idea and beat us to it.

About an hour later we emerge, not because we're any the wiser for searching our phones for breaking news, or texts from Logan, but because of the slow lifting of our fear when nothing happens, no shots, no screams, just that constant drone of the *Pink Panther* theme over the hidden speakers, along with "Calcutta" by Lawrence Welk, and a few other elevator music tunes that seem so bizarrely out of place.

The casino floor is now eerily deserted.

The Vegas Strip and every hotel and casino within walking distance of the Mandalay Bay is on lockdown. No one, except guests, is allowed in. No one, guests or otherwise, is allowed out. Having no idea when the order will be lifted—it could be all night or longer for all we know—Omar, Jenny, Paula, and I rent rooms at the Aria. They offer us reduced rates because of the state of emergency.

The first thing Paula does, when we get to our room, is turn on the TV to the local news. The first thing I do is call Nate at the Monte Carlo. Landline to landline. Direct to his room. He answers groggily.

"Yeah?"

I am so relieved to hear his voice, *just* to hear his voice, that I don't respond right away.

"Who is this?" he says.

"It's me," I say. "You're in your room. That's all that matters."

"What're you talking about?"

Until now it hasn't occurred to me that Nate could possibly have slept through this entire ordeal, but apparently that's the case.

On TV, the newscaster says that at least twenty people are confirmed dead. The ticker tape running at the bottom of the screen reports that officials found bomb-making material, ammonium nitrate, in Stephen Paddock's car. This is the key ingredient in the Oklahoma City bombing that killed 168 people.

"There was a horrible shooting on the Strip. Everything's shut down. I'm just calling," I say, "to make sure you're all right."

"Jesus, Dad, it's one o'clock in the morning. I'll call you back in a few hours."

Then he hangs up, leaving me to wonder if he is simply too sleepy and disoriented to grasp the significance of what I told him, or if his reaction is one particular to his generation, who've grown up with terrorism, multiple wars abroad, Columbine-like massacres, gangland killings, civil unrest and riots, and the constant barrage of Amber Alerts on our freeway signs. Maybe, after a while, all the violence and insanity merges into a single common pool of blood that merits no special distinction.

Paula and I lie in bed and watch the news.

By 2:30 a.m., she is asleep.

By 3:30 a.m., I am still awake, and fifty people are now said to be dead, with more than two hundred injured. Around four that morning, President Trump tweets his condolences to the victims and their families, and I turn off the TV.

I try to sleep but cannot.

My medication, Seroquel, is in my suitcase at the Monte Carlo, and without it my brain speeds up. Without it, should I fall asleep, there is no telling where my head will take me. My fear of nightmares is in and of itself enough to keep me wide awake. Seroquel is an antipsychotic typically prescribed for mental illnesses ranging from schizophrenia to bipolar disorder, depression, PTSD, and aggression, and for me it's a miracle drug, providing much-needed relief from several of these afflictions. I've been taking it for close to fifteen years. My system has become dependent on it, and if I miss a single dose, which I must take every evening before bed, my thoughts spin out of control. One second I'll fixate on something that happened fifty years ago, some childhood memory, and the next I'm plotting the demise of someone who recently wronged me. My energy level rockets. I can feel my muscles tense, my arms and legs itch and tingle, and I want to *move*. I want to *go* places. *Do* things. Lying in bed with my eyes closed requires extraordinary concentration, and I have to tell myself repeatedly that I'm supposed to be tired, I'm supposed to rest.

The clock on the nightstand reads 5:05 a.m., and I have to fight the urge not to wake Paula and say come on, get up, let's go to breakfast.

The last time I remember checking the clock, before I nod off, it's 6:28 a.m. I wake up about an hour later to the smell of coffee, and, thankfully, I have no memory of any nightmares. I hear water running. Paula is in the shower. The TV is on, the sound off. The ticker tape scrolls along the bottom of the screen. The death toll has risen to fifty-eight. Over five hundred others are reported injured.

We all meet for breakfast at the Hard Rock Cafe. It's across the street from the Monte Carlo, and in walking there I'm surprised that the Strip is already packed with tourists and locals. Young men hawk self-made hip-hop CDs. Other peddlers hand out passes to strip clubs, tickets for free drinks, and pamphlets advertising trips to the Grand Canyon. The only change from last night to now is that they are not as aggressive, cutting you off as you try to step around them, waving their goods and offers in your face. This morning a sickly pallor hangs over the Strip, and everyone seems to know, without speaking a word about it, that this is not the time or place to go about business as usual, though that is what we are trying to do. Paula, Logan, his girlfriend, Nate, and I, we all set out to have a good time in Vegas, catch up, tell stories, laugh, and now it's as if, in a state of shock, we are just going through the motions.

Without my medication, and with so little sleep, my energy soon wanes, and I feel almost as if I had gotten drunk the night before. That I'm hungover. There's a dull, steady pounding in my head. If not for Logan, since we see so little of each other, I would've returned to my room that morning, doubled up on my medication, and climbed back into bed. The beauty of Vegas hotels is that they understand the importance of darkness. No matter what time of day, when you pull the drapes shut, it might as well be the dead of night. This is ideal for around-the-clock gamblers and drunks the likes of Stephen Paddock. This is also ideal for people who miss their dose of psych meds as well as those who should be on them—like Paddock, or better yet, institutionalized long before he could act out his homicidal fantasies.

After breakfast, we stop and mingle with the crowd along a pedestrian overpass that offers a good view of the Mandalay Bay. It's just a couple of blocks away. We can see the two windows missing from the suite on the thirty-second floor. Below, on the street, the Las Vegas Police have cordoned off the sidewalks with yellow tape. Big orange traffic barriers block the intersection and there are cruisers surrounding the entire area around the hotel. People on the overpass snap pictures with their cells. One girl with a sleeve of tats has found a site on her phone with a tinny recording of the massacre, and I can hear it, weakly, the sound of gunshots and screams. I think of the injured. I think of the dead and those who survive them. Mothers and fathers. Siblings. Family. Friends. The sorrow and torment. At night they will no longer be able to sleep. Visions will jolt them awake. The keening and cries will echo in their minds for the rest of their lives. It is irreversible, this haunting, and for me to believe that somehow the dead are more fortunate is a perversion, for there is no greater robbery than the taking of life.

While Courtney and my family continue to look at the murder scene, I look at Logan for telltale signs of alcoholism. Is his face bloated? No. Are his eyes bloodshot? No. The sun is shining hard on us, and so I look for sweat on his brow and neck, because alcoholics retain fluids, and when we overheat we sweat heavily. But he is not sweating. I think about our breakfast. Did he seem moody? Sluggish? Logan likes Western wear, cowboy boots, and the silver belt buckles he's earned from rodeos, riding broncs and bulls, and this type, or stereotype, is well-known for alcoholic drinking.

He deals with hardcore criminals, psychotics, and sociopaths on a daily basis, so it's not as if he doesn't sense that I'm staring at him. Staying alive for my boy means staying alert, as does anticipating people's worst intentions, which is to say he's aware of his surroundings at all times.

"What're you looking at me for?"

"I'm not looking at you," I say.

He shakes his head at me.

"You've been eyeballing me this whole trip. I'm fine, okay? I got drunk with Courtney the first night I got here, after training, and then I had that one glass of wine at dinner last night. That's it."

"Are you guys arguing?" Paula says.

Now they all turn away from the Mandalay Bay and stare at us.

"We're fine," I say.

I nod to Logan and start to walk. He follows. We stop when I know they won't be able to hear us.

"I hardly see you anymore," I say. "I'm not being mean. I'm your dad. I worry."

A man with a long gray ponytail, his face weathered from the sun, is taping crosses made of cardboard and painted white on the side of the overpass. We have to step back. We have to make room for him to do his work.

"I know," Logan says. "I get it. Let me put it this way. I have a fifth of Jack in my kitchen cupboard and it's been there since May."

It's a good answer but it doesn't necessarily alleviate my concerns.

"What about my visit last year?"

"I apologized for that already. I got worked up that night, and I'm not saying it's gone, but I definitely don't get drunk over it anymore."

He's seen blood, lots of it, and he's not good with it. But I also know he's seen more since we last saw each other and he's told me that it gets easier. I'd like to believe him, but I've experienced things, too, and I drank over them for the better part of my life, or at least I used them as an excuse to drink. I had all kinds of excuses. None of the things I wanted to blank out got easier with time, and because they didn't, I have trouble believing that my son is telling the truth. It's hard for me to give him or anyone the benefit of the doubt because as a drunk I lied so often, particularly to those I love most, that I stopped believing in myself.

So, rightly or wrongly, I project.

"Honestly?"

"Honestly," he says.

"Come here," I say.

I hug all of my boys. I make a point of telling them how proud I am of them, and when we have to say goodbye, I kiss them on the cheek. Sometimes I'll kiss them on both cheeks. This is how my father used to say goodbye to me, but I'll never know if his eyes started to burn, as mine sometimes do a couple hours later. This is after Logan and Courtney are gone, heading back to Wyoming.

Checkout is at eleven, and we're in the car by then, leaving Las Vegas. We're on the highway passing through the Mojave Desert. The land is dry and barren except for some sagebrush and tumbleweed. In the rearview mirror, I see Nate staring at his cell phone. Playing a game? Conducting business? Paula looks over at me.

"Are you crying?"

"It's allergies," I say. "My eyes burn."

"You don't have allergies."

"The doctor said I was allergic to sagebrush. Look out there. What do you see?"

"The doctors diagnosed you with all kinds of stuff," she says, "but not allergies." Paula punches me in the arm. "I know you miss him, but you'll see him again."

I am allergic to sagebrush, but the windows are rolled up. The air conditioner is on, so I suppose a case could be made that the pollens aren't getting into the cab. That it isn't the cause of the watery eyes. I suppose it could also be that I'll miss him, as any parent would his child when they go their separate ways. But of course there will be a next time. Of course there will always be a next time. It just can't be possible that I'm taking anything for granted each time we part, the very moment I look away.

Apology to the Young Addict

You post your picture on Facebook. It's a close-up. Your long hair is dark brown. On one side you have strands of it curled behind your ear. Your eyes are dark brown, too, but they are also glossy and red. In your hand is a glass pipe, the bowl hot and alive, swirling with gray smoke. You're holding it out to whoever is taking the picture, but it looks as if you're offering it to me. And in a way, I suppose, that's exactly what you're doing. One of my sons went to high school with you and tells me that you had a reputation for using drugs. By your junior year, he says you're MIA, and I'm guessing you dropped out or moved off the mountain. Either way I don't see or hear about you again until your picture pops up on Facebook.

You must be about twenty now. I lose track of time. In the beginning, as a child, you probably wonder why, when I come to see your father, he always asks you to go to your room and watch TV or take the dogs for a walk. After a while, though, and I don't suppose it takes more than a few visits, you must catch on. By no means am I his only friend, if you can call his many visitors *friends*, because truthfully we are not. Sure, we laugh and joke and talk too long, like friends do, but we always leave looking and acting differently than when we arrived. Sometimes we move in slow motion. Sometimes we're fidgety and nervous. It depends on the drug, whether it's a stimulant or depressant. Heroin or coke. Or meth. Or all three for an interesting little cocktail. And then you detect that strange smell in the air that not even our cigarette smoke can mask, and it's not marijuana, either. That odor you know well because everyone in junior high is smoking it, or almost everyone, and maybe you've even sampled it yourself already. But this other odor, it's different, a chemical odor, kind of like burning rubber. It's hard to describe but it smells nothing like weed.

Other times your father's friends come and go so quickly you must wonder why they ever bothered to visit. Some of us meet him at the door and a minute later we're back in our cars.

Your mother, where's she?

When did you last see her? I'm not familiar with this part of your story, knowing only that she's not there for you at this point in your life. She's an addict, too, this much I do know, and maybe she's still using when your father is clean. Maybe that's why she left. If this is the case, at least with your father you have a roof over your head and food in the refrigerator. At least with him you attend school instead of bouncing from one dope house to another, crashing on beat-up couches or dirty floors, and sometimes, when your mother wears out her welcome, having to sleep on the streets.

To be fair, your father has seven years clean from heroin and cocaine before he receives his disability settlement for an injury he suffers working as a heavy equipment operator. He undergoes spinal fusion surgery but the procedure is hardly successful in re-lieving his pain. Still, for those seven years, he refuses the Vicodin and Oxycodone the doctors prescribe, knowing it will trigger his old cravings, and even though he walks slowly, wincing often, he nonetheless manages to take you fishing off the docks in Lake Arrowhead. You remember he's good at it, and teaches you how to be good at it, too, so that you both catch plenty of trout and bass. You also remember him taking you camping and how comforting, how calming, how secure and safe and loved you feel snuggling up to him in your sleeping bags in the tent he shows you how to pitch, because he can't do much of the work himself. You like helping him. You like knowing he needs you, as you need him, and you think of you and your father as a little team. Together you can take on the world.

But money can be a trigger, too.

For the addict it can weaken the resolve to stay clean. It can give you a false sense of liberation. Why this is, I don't know for certain, but I've seen it happen too often not to believe there's truth in it—addicts and alcoholics struggling to make ends meet, and then, when the burden is lifted, finding themselves drunk or strung out again. A seventy-five-thousand-dollar disability set-tlement is a windfall when you've been living month to month on paltry government disability checks.

Ironically your father is my first sponsor, once a week taking me through the Big Book line by line, page by page, but after one too many slips I give up on myself and he gives up on me, too. I can't blame him. We stop seeing each other until he calls out of the blue one day, asks if I'm clean, and when I tell him I'm not, that I'm drinking as we speak, he laughs and invites me over. He has it all. Heroin. Coke. Plenty of booze. From that night on we party hard and often, but your father is diligent, always cautious never to let you catch us in the act of getting high. He makes certain that his drugs and paraphernalia are always well hidden and never brought out until they're needed. Syringes. A couple spoons, the hollow part blackened, the handles bent for better control, easier balance. One tourniquet is an old leather belt with teeth marks on the strap. The other is easy to tie, a length of rubber tubing, but hard to unknot with one hand, especially when you're high.

You aren't supposed to be there.

You are, instead, supposed to be spending the night with a friend. I don't know the full story, if your friend gets sick or you have a fight and want to come home early, but I remember that you couldn't have been more than eleven or twelve years old, and that we don't hear you unlock the front door. We don't hear your footsteps on the stairs leading to the living room where your father and I sit on the couch beside a coffee table scattered with syringes and booze and little baggies of heroin and coke. I'm already deep on the nod, melting into the couch. Your father has just tied off his arm, biting down on the leather strap with his teeth, searching for a vein. He slips the needle in and presses the plunger. Blood slides down his forearm and you drop the backpack that's hanging from your shoulder. It hits the floor and a pair of pajamas with little blue flowers on them tumble out. Your eyes meet with your father's and I lower mine.

"Baby," he says. "I'm sorry. Come here."

He tries to get up from the couch but falls back. The heroin is strong and his injuries make standing even harder. He tries again and succeeds this time, though he's shaky on his feet. You run to your room, slam and lock the door. Your father weaves down the hallway, calling your name, and when I hear you crying, I pick up my cigarettes and lighter and leave. There is no excuse, accidental or otherwise, for an adult to use narcotics in front of a child, and my presence alone that night makes me complicit in your addiction today.

I am and am not guilty.

I am and am not responsible.

Jump in time. Fast-forward a few years. Your father is pulled over for a broken taillight and ends up getting arrested for possession and distribution of narcotics. By no means is this his first run-in with the law. Once, traveling through Texas, he's busted with two kilos of heroin and spends four years in the state prison in Huntsville, best known for the most active execution chamber in the United States. This time the judge sends him to Glen Helen in San Bernardino County. One day, in another life, I will find myself speaking to the convicts here about drug and alcohol abuse.

In his midforties, he is, like myself, no longer a young man, and while serving the first year of his two-year sentence he suffers a massive heart attack. The doctors save him with triple bypass surgery, and I'm sure they warn him that if he uses drugs again it will be his last heart attack. But when has the fear of death ever stopped an addict? Isn't it, in some ways, what we're really searching for? Isn't it, in some ways, what we really want? Certainly it's an answer to the end of the misery called addiction and all the shame and anguish and self-loathing that's killing us anyway.

Your father used to say, "You can always put more in but you can't take it out," which means the wise addict, if there is such a thing, is conservative and cautious. You know when you buy Jack Daniel's that you're getting eighty proof Tennessee whiskey. On every bottle there's a government seal that states exactly that and we have officials that regularly inspect their distilleries. But there are no standards or quality control when you buy dope. One day your dealer might sell you weak or bunk product. A week later it might be stellar, so the same amount you shot last time might kill you now. What happens, though, when you have a weak heart and *any* dose, even a small one, is enough to put you under? That's the case with your father when he's released and inside of a month he dies of what the coroner concludes is an overdose.

Here's the ugliest part.

Here's the scene where trauma gives you a choice. Embrace the darkness or run from it. Break the cycle or join it. I can't and won't blame you, as I have no right, because I made the wrong choice, too, when I was young and lost my brother. My sister did the same and also found herself an early grave.

That little team, just your father and you, it's true. He had only you. All other family ties had been ruined and severed long ago, and so who do his so-called friends phone when they can't revive him? Not the paramedics. Paramedics bring police and police make arrests. Bring him to hospital? That's also risky. Besides, by then, he's probably stopped breathing. Instead, like good junkies concerned only for themselves, they gather up their dope, scales, pipes, syringes—all the accouterments of addiction—call you, and get out of whosever house or apartment they're in. I bet they even rifled through his pockets before they left. I'm told the message is brief.

"Come get your father."

They give you an address and hang up. I have a hard time believing the caller would tell you he's dead. I don't suppose it's fair to generalize, but junkies are notorious for being liars, cowards, and thieves.

So let me add it up.

You're just a kid the first time we meet and your father and I go on a hard run. Then he spends two years in prison while I begin the arduous, drawn-out struggle to clean up my act. That should make you about seventeen or eighteen when you pull up to the house or apartment in your father's old truck, the one he gave you after he lost his license and went to prison again. Maybe you're thinking that he's passed out drunk. Possibly you detect the panic in the caller's voice and already suspect the worst. I doubt it, though, and it has nothing to do with your youth. Old or young, clean or dirty, even the most jaded among us cling to hope where we know there is none.

I understand you go there alone.

I understand the door is left unlocked, so all you have to do is turn the knob and walk inside and this is how you find him, sprawled out on the couch in the living room, his face pale blue, his limbs already stiffening. I don't know if you drew back in terror or kneeled by his side and cried and held him and kissed his cold skin. That's as far as I let imagination invade this private and heartbreaking moment of your life.

Under your picture on Facebook, in the reply box, I write that *it doesn't have to be this way*, knowing full well my words mean nothing. I can hear you laughing. I can see you shaking your head and saying:

"You motherfucker, of all people, slamming dope with my dad and now this shit. Fuck you. Of course it has to be this way. How could it be any other?"

And maybe you're right. Maybe this motherfucker might as well have snapped your picture. Fuck his laments, you think. Fuck his apologies. You hate the hypocrisy of reformed addicts telling you that the dope will stop working one day, that it always does, and in the end you'll be left with nothing but misery. That you'll do things you never imagined yourself capable of doing. Sell your body. Rip off friends and whatever family you might still have left.

This is only the beginning.

What the older recovering addict has to offer the younger, active addict is the hope and promise of change through example and really nothing more.

Listen.

I despise him, too, but at least for today he is as dead as your father, and hopefully he will remain dead, this old junkie staring into the photo of your glossy red eyes, who long ago might just as well have passed that glowing hot pipe to you.

A God of My Understanding

I'm seven years old the night I look up at the sky and all its stars and shake my fist and curse God. Of course I expect to instantly be struck dead, and when nothing happens, it confirms my belief that He does not exist. Or, if He does, He certainly doesn't care about us. Our mother is in prison, and every night for months and months my older sister and I kneel at the foot of my bed and pray together, thanking God for all the good things in our life and imploring Him to *please* return our mother to us. Then she tucks me in, kisses me on the forehead, and turns out the lights.

How often do we have to plead?

How often do we have to beg before our prayers are answered? After a while I begin to think maybe He isn't there. Maybe He doesn't consider us worthy of His attention. At the very least He isn't listening, and Marilyn and I are wasting our time asking for His help. So one night, when she tells me to kneel with her and pray, I refuse.

"Why?" she says.

"Because He isn't there."

"You don't know that."

"And you don't know He is."

"But you have to believe, Jimmy. Everything happens for a reason. God has a plan for all of us," she tells me, "including Mom."

I'm not buying it.

Every Sunday Marilyn takes me to a Lutheran church. I find it boring, the sermons and hymns, but I love my sister and I know she needs my company and support. I know she needs to feel that she is helping us both. That she is not alone in her beliefs. Our father, though baptized Methodist and a believer in Christ, doesn't much like church. He thinks there are too many hypocrites there, so he won't go with us, and our older brother, a precocious fourteen-year-old, has already read and embraced the works of several atheist and agnostic philosophers. I don't want to hurt my sister but I also don't want to pray anymore, because it isn't working, or to go to church and be bored, or to believe in something I can't see or hear or touch.

Mostly, though, I am angry that our mother is in prison. Despite sharing the same sense of loss and grief, my sister, brother, and I are cut off from one another and trapped in our own private hell. The night I refuse to kneel and turn away from my sister and run outside and look up at the sky and all its stars and shake my fist and say *fuck you, God* is the night I give up on faith and prayer and this idea that He is in control of our lives. That everything happens for a reason. From here on out, until my early forties, when asked if I believe in God, I recoil and say, with the same piousness as a religious zealot, that I am an atheist.

In my twenties, while in college studying English, I have a

philosophy professor who assigns readings from Nietzsche, Sartre, and Schopenhauer, among others. From time to time, although it's not exactly part of the curriculum, my literature professors let it be known how little they regard religion, particularly Christianity. By the time I graduate I discover that I'm remarkably more intelligent than anyone who did not have the good fortune to attend an institution of higher learning—and of those who did, and who still cling to their foolish beliefs, they are a pathetic lot hardly worthy of my attention. I'm especially convinced of my stunning intellect when I drink, as drinking makes me smarter, or so I like to think, and at this juncture in life I've begun to drink daily. Drunk or sober, however, I nonetheless relish each and every opportunity to exercise my extraordinary reasoning abilities debating those pitifully dim-witted people of faith.

God?

Prove it. You can't. Logic wins every time, but if you still insist on talking about religion, well, let's begin with all the hate it inspires, all the harm it causes, all the millions killed in the name of the Almighty. Christianity is just another word for murder and war. If that's the God you want to embrace you're one twisted soul, assuming there is such a thing as a soul, which is in and of itself the stuff of fantasy and conjecture. I do not for a second consider that historically Christians may also have saved millions of lives through acts of kindness and charity. No. I reject such possibilities as nothing more than supposition and fallacy.

Every misfortune in my life only reaffirms my belief that we're all on our own in this cruel world. But should I somehow happen to be wrong, though I'm certain I am not, but if in the off chance He *does* exist, why doesn't He step up to the plate and prevent major calamities? War? Natural disasters? Fires and floods? And what of the toddler riddled with cancer or the baby born with hideous defects? What of the child that dies in a hit-and-run at the hands of a drunk driver? Where the hell is He when shit hits the fan? At best, if He's not a cruel God, He's an indifferent one, and what good is a God like that? If He's there, I resent Him for his failings, and if He's not, then what's to care about?

I feel the same about my drinking.

Who cares if I get drunk or high? What difference does it make how I live my life? Morals are relative. What you think is good I may think is bad. And vice versa. Don't judge me with your religious zealotry and I won't judge you, though of course I do.

Wise up. Have fun.

Do what you want. The moment we're born is the moment we begin digging our own graves, so cut loose. Enjoy yourself anyway you like. Life is entrapment by death and the clock is running out.

Through the years, as my alcoholism gets worse, I nonetheless believe that I am in complete control of my life. I *choose* to raise that bottle to my lips. I *choose* to pop that pill, snort that powder, or stick that needle in my arm. Of course I can quit any time I want, when I want, I just *don't want*. Those zealots preach that God has given us free will, but when you're talking booze and narcotics, once we decide to use and abuse, that decision may well lead to a foregone conclusion, robbing us of the power of choice. Logic and reason fly out the window when it comes to addiction, as they do with this crazy notion of God, and if you think that willpower alone can save your sorry ass, good luck to you.

But I'm a stubborn man.

If, and this is a big *if,* I do on occasion overindulge, it's because my wife won't shut up about it. It's because the kids stress me out. It's because I work hard all day and I'm entitled to a couple of drinks when I come home or decide instead to stop off at a bar. That that couple of drinks is actually a dozen or better, usually better, is meaningless in a meaningless world. Some stumble and slur their words after two or three drinks while others, such as myself, barely get buzzed. These are just a few of the things that I tell myself when rationalizing my drinking and using, and I do all sorts of rationalizing along my merry way to self-destruction.

For the sake of brevity I'll skip over the many times I've passed out and come to in places where I have no idea how I got there. Someone's garage. The parking lot behind a dumpster of a liquor store. My own front yard. I'll skip over that exciting night when I'm stabbed twice in the back with a screwdriver over a drug deal gone bad, as well as the thrilling times I get my nose broken, not once but on three separate occasions. I'll also skip the time some lowlife puts a gun to my head and pulls the trigger and it jams. I'll skip the time I shoot heroin with our southern neighbors who can't speak a word of English and deal in kilos, ARs, grenades, and other munitions. Who cares if we can't talk to each other so long as the dope is good and plentiful? And I'll skip the occasion where I party with members of the Aryan Brothers who threaten to bury me in the desert outside Hesperia when I let it slip that my stepmother is Mexican. Race. Ethics. Morals. They mean little to the alcoholic-addict. Zero, exactly, when dope is involved.

Most troubling, I'll skip the many nights I traumatize my children with drunken, violent outbursts while fighting with my wife and doing and saying cruel and hurtful things for which I'll never forgive myself. And, finally, I'll skip the part nearing the end of my drinking and drugging career where I visit a dear old friend from high school who is fully stocked and we drink and shoot pharmaceutical morphine sulfate and snort speed and I still can't seem to get high.

The drugs just plain stop working.

Try as I might, short of OD'ing, I can't get out of my head, and the goal is and always has been to shut the brain down. The whole idea behind getting wasted is to escape my thoughts and emotions, because I don't like how I think and feel. Frankly, if the truth be known, I don't much like *myself*, but if I can't depend on drugs and alcohol to take me where I want to go, which is oblivion, then how do I get relief from the misery that consumes me?

Eventually I find myself alone and lost in this dank, ugly place of despair where the idea of checking out strikes me as perfectly reasonable. What's more sensible than suicide when you can't kick your pain and anguish any more than you can the drugs and booze you use to escape those feelings? Why not complete the family circle?

It's all about diminishing returns. It's all about cutting your losses, and I'd cut them in a heartbeat if I didn't worry that my wife and children might forever torment themselves wondering if they had anything to do with it, if they could've somehow saved me, just as I did over the loss of my brother and sister. But I'm not so far gone as to not have a conscience. There is, in short, a great deal to skip over before I finally come to realize, and I speak only for myself, that maybe I should give this God thing a try. At the very least, since all my previous attempts to get clean and sober have ended in failure, I ought to open my mind to the possibility that there is, as they say in Alcoholics Anonymous, a Power greater than ourselves. I still know I'm too smart for God, but I also know that doing it my way is working like a pinball machine, with me as the ball, bouncing back and forth between sobriety and drunkenness, hitting the bumpers, riding the railings, and then invariably, inevitably, missing the shot and ending up right back in the gutter.

I spend a decade going in and out of the rooms of A.A., along with an occasional stint in rehab, before I'm able to broach that ridiculous idea of God. It's only been a few months since I've come off the bender with my dear old friend from high school when I meet with my sponsor, Nick, at our usual spot, Bill's Diner, near the A.A. club in the little mountain town of Blue Jay. We're having coffee. We've just been to a meeting. It's night.

"You admit you're an alcoholic?"

"Yeah."

"And your life is unmanageable."

"Yeah.

"Then you got Step One down," he says.

"I think so."

"Either you do or you don't. No ands, ifs, or buts."

"I do."

"But you're stuck on Step Two?"

"It's the Higher Power part," I say. "I don't believe in God."

Nick takes a sip of his coffee and sets it on the saucer. He looks me in the eye.

"Tell you what, just start praying," he says. "Once a day. Ten times or twenty. I don't care. Whenever the thought of a drink pops into your head, I want you to drop to your knees and pray like a sonofabitch."

"To what?"

He shrugs.

"Whatever you want. The Great Spirit in the Sky. Zeus. A doorknob. I don't give a shit. You just have to accept that you're not in charge of this messed-up world. And trust me on this, Jim, you're not."

The running joke in A.A. is that if you're having trouble buying into the God thing then make your Higher Power the doorknob to your A.A. club, so you're reminded, every time you come in and out of meetings, that the knob exists and your sobriety depends on turning it.

Fake it, they say, until you make it.

Though I've always thought it was stupid, this notion of lying to yourself until you believe the lie, I'm desperate enough to hold my tongue and consider my options, which at this point seem somewhat limited. Either I give up and continue drinking and using to the bitter end. Or I give up and listen to my sponsor. I've burned through all of my own ideas, including, as it states in the A.A. Big Book, *countless attempts* to control my drinking by restricting it to weekends, for instance, or working out more at the gym. Or never drinking in the mornings. All of my best efforts, however, always fall short of the mark.

So I pray.

I pray at night before I go to bed. I pray in my office at school before I go to class. I pray after I finish teaching for the day and I'm stressed out and my nerves are shot and I really, really need that drink. My hands are shaking. I'm queasy. My face is hot and sweaty, and there I am, kneeling in my office before a stack of student essays piled on my desk, asking under my breath, asking quietly, asking desperately for this Thing, whatever it is, to please relieve me of the obsession to drink. Of course I feel silly talking to what I'm convinced is nothing, but incredibly, unbelievably, my hands stop shaking. The queasiness passes, and at least for today, at least for this night, the need to drink is lifted. It's bizarre. And it seems to work for a while, but then I screw up again, and things get even crazier.

I don't know if I fall off the wagon because I'm not attending enough meetings or praying hard enough, if I just wanted relief from the struggle to *not* drink, or if, frankly, I let those easy rationalizations creep back into my head—that life is pointless, that in the vastness of this great cosmos who cares if I get drunk or high.

I am nothing.

I mean nothing. The world is nothing. Your time on this planet is but a blink of the eye. Less. There are two little voices in my head, one telling me not to think this way, that you have people who love you and whom you love, that life matters, that *you matter*, while this other voice is saying knock off the kumbaya shit and have a drink, a line, shoot some dope. You're a miserable creature on a miserable planet, so quit this sobriety nonsense and do what you do best. Get wasted. If I let that second voice roll around up there in my head for more than a minute or two, I'm a goner, off and running like a racehorse out of the gates.

The details of my last big bender are trivial in light of the foul weather and the windy mountain highway that I have to drive to get home on this wonderfully strange and dangerous night many years ago. I can no more recall how much I drank as where I drank it. One bar or five? All I know is that I'd been good up until then. I'd been sober a few months, but once I get a taste of it, literally a couple sips, I start downing drinks as if I'm trying to make up for all the booze I lost out on when I stopped. For a mere mortal, it would be a lethal dose, a trip to the ER, but of course as a well-trained, experienced drunk, albeit a little rusty from my layoff, I'm convinced that I'm an exception to the rule. Though I couldn't possibly walk a straight line if a peace officer kindly asked me to do so, I feel perfectly cable of operating heavy machinery, in this case a three-quarter-ton Dodge pickup with a burned-out headlight. I'm convinced that the problem is not so much my state of mind, or lack thereof, as it is the fog that envelops the mountain highway. Drunk or sober, on the worst of nights, and this is one of worst, you can't see ten feet ahead of you. The drop-off, as you rise from the desert flatlands of San Bernardino into the pines, reaches thousands of feet, and the slightest miscalculation, the smallest nudge of the wheel, an inch to one side or the other, can send you sailing over the edge, plummeting end over end to your death.

Many a driver has met his fate on this highway in exactly this manner. Wiser ones often pull into one of the turnouts and sleep in their cars until the fog lifts. I am, however, anything but wise: I am risking not only my life navigating this treacherous stretch of highway shrouded in dense, impenetrable fog, but the lives of others as well. Drunk driving is an act of selfishness. And as a drunk I am a selfish, self-centered person, and so I proceed stupidly, recklessly, with no regard for the safety or well-being of my fellow man. Covering one eye with my hand, so I won't see double of the double yellow line, or double the single white one on the right, is a safety technique you won't find in the State of California's driver's manual. It is instead the lore of alcoholics, based on tried-and-true experience and passed down through the generations from one drunk to another. The mere possession of such knowledge, this trick of the trade, is justifiably cause for alarm, shock, and disgust to the responsible, nonalcoholic citizenry, as would be opening your door a crack so you can see the double-double yellow line in relation to your front tire. A few miles up the road I come within inches of rear-ending an eighteen-wheeler whose driver had parked in the middle of the highway with his bright red emergency flashers on. In this blinding fog, however, the lights are hardly bright even when I'm right on top of them. A couple miles later my truck dips, lunging toward the edge of the cliff. My front tire spins freely in the air, and I think to myself, "Oh shit, what a way to go," because I'm going, there's no doubt about it. Luckily, my rear tire is still grounded, and with a quick turn of the wheel I'm back on the road. Seconds later a deer freezes in my one working headlight, and when I veer to avoid running over the poor thing, I find myself in the opposite lane leading down the mountain. I hear a horn before I spot the headlights and swerve out of the way just in the nick of time. Even though we were both going slow, a direct head-on at most any speed translates to twisted steel, shattered glass, blood, and broken bones.

I've driven drunk thousands of times without a single DUI or wreck. Maybe I've had a few close calls here and there, lightly scraping the side of my car on one of those steel posts in a parking lot, say, tapping another car's bumper or gently grazing its fender, but nothing serious has ever happened. The worst case was knocking off the side mirror of a school bus, but that wasn't my fault, I thought at the time, because the driver hadn't pulled completely off the road when he stopped to let the children off. Never have I attributed my driving drunk without consequence to anything other than my exceptional motor skills. But on this night on this foggy highway, when I reach the top of the mountain and pull over to catch my breath, I sense a presence beside me.

I don't know what it is.

I look over at the passenger's seat. There's nothing there. But I *feel it*, an actual physical presence. Then I hear a voice. Not in my head, either. This is a *real* voice.

"I'm here," it says.

It's not loud but the words are clear and the tone is calm. I wait.

I listen for more.

I can still feel its presence. I want to hear the voice, though, to be sure, so I wait longer, and I'm still waiting, even today.

Bill Wilson, cofounder of Alcoholics Anonymous, credits the psychologist and philosopher Carl Jung as saying that the only hope of sobriety for the seemingly hopeless drunk is a religious experience. In the Big Book of A.A., Bill changed it to a *spiritual* experience, and recalls how, in the depths of a suicidal depression, he cries out, "'If there is a God, let him show himself! I am ready to do anything, anything' [and] suddenly the room lit up with a great white light. I was caught up into an ecstasy which there are no words to describe."

I didn't see any great white light and I certainly wasn't ecstatic. If anything I was stunned and confused, but after a while I started thinking that that voice suggested more than it just being there for me on that one foggy night. All those close calls I survived, from partying with the AB and the Mexican drug and arms dealers to having a gun put to my head and it jamming, I always attributed to luck. Or chance. Or, better still, crediting myself as a badass who could run with the best of the baddest.

Fact is, I am no badass.

I'm a soft, aging college professor with a drug and alcohol problem, and when I think about it, when I think really hard and deeply, I can remember feeling that presence a few times before. It isn't until I *heard it* that I started wondering how it is that I'm still alive when I should've been dead a hundred times over.

"I'm here," it says, which means, I've come to believe, that maybe I've never been alone.

After that incident on the foggy highway, when I get a couple days of sobriety under my belt, I meet with Nick at our local Starbucks instead of the diner. Of course he already knows I messed up just by looking at me. I'm haggard and hungover and anyone could see the guilt on my face, so he cuts to the quick.

"Was it fun?" he says.

"Oh yeah, lots of fun. I almost killed myself trying to drive home in that crazy fog we had last week."

"But you didn't. You got another chance. You don't know how many people I've sponsored over the years who go out and never make it back. One guy climbed up into a tree and shot himself in the face. A.A.," he says, "once you get a taste of it, really screws with your high."

Then I tell him about the voice I heard, shaking my head as I talk as if I'm admitting, without directly saying so, that I know I'm totally out of my mind.

"Auditory hallucinations," I say. "I was so drunk I was hearing stuff."

"Really?" he says.

"Really."

"So it was all in your head," he says. "Neurons misfiring. Crazy neurons."

"Yeah," I say. "Crazy neurons."

Nick leans back in his seat and rubs his chin between his fingers.

"Hmm," he says. "Just for the sake of argument, what if it wasn't? Say maybe what you heard was real. Say maybe you opened the door a crack."

"What door?"

"You've been praying, right?"

"Not that night."

"But before, you've been praying. And when you pray," he says, "whether you believe or not, you let your guard down. And when you let your guard down, even a little, belief can creep in. And when belief creeps in, all bets are off. You might see things you never saw before. You might hear things you never heard before. Because you aren't listening," he says, "doesn't mean you haven't been spoken to. Because you aren't looking doesn't mean something isn't there." He pauses. He smiles. "Sounds to me like you might've had yourself a spiritual experience."

"But I was *drunk*."

"That does throw a wrench into things. But you still can never tell. Drunk or high, you might've heard right. Maybe," he says, and he says exactly what I've been thinking, "you've never been alone."

This is and is not what I want him to say. It's so much easier to reject the unexplainable than to embrace it and run the risk of being labeled crazy, or worse, a stupid, irrational believer in the greatest sham in the history of mankind. How can any reasonable, halfway intelligent, college-educated person accept the hearing of an inexplicable voice as evidence of anything other than a simple alcoholic hallucination? After all, don't schizophrenics hear voices, and I've been diagnosed by two different shrinks of having a mild case of it, along with borderline personality disorder, and manic depression, my preferred term for the more popular euphemism of bipolarism, which hardly describes the true nature of the illness. My sponsor, kind man that he is, is only humoring me.

So with a renewed, albeit still questionable vigor, I return to prayer.

I am sick and tired, as they say in A.A., of being sick and tired. I am sick and tired of getting sober for a few days, a few weeks, sometimes a couple months, once a little over six, and then sadly, regrettably, screwing up and getting drunk yet again.

Part of the problem, I think, is that I'm not being diligent enough with the Steps. I'm not practicing them on a daily basis. Another part, however, is that I still don't know to what or whom to pray. Nick says to pray to a God of my own understanding, as it's preached in A.A., but I can't help but balk at the idea of making up my own God. It feels like I'm praying to nothing and that's what I'm trying to get away from. The nothingness. That life is nothing. That I am nothing. There's an emptiness inside me that so badly needs to be filled, and when you take away the drugs and alcohol I've been trying to fill it with, I don't know where to begin. When I try the Great Spirit in the Sky thing, images

of redwood trees and rivers and Native Americans keep popping
into my head, and as much as I love Mother Nature I feel like a
fraud praying to Her. Zeus doesn't do it for me, either, and the
doorknob thing is ridiculous. This is where my sister's early childhood attempts to brainwash me come back into play.

One night, as I'm kneeling at my bedside, giving it my best
shot, I find myself quietly repeating the old words my sister forced
me to memorize: "Our Father who art in heaven, hallowed be Thy
name, Thy kingdom come, Thy will be done . . ." And while I'm
finishing up, my mind fixates on the image of Christ in his last
moments on the cross, spikes driven through his hands and feet,
blood seeping from the wounds, his head adorned with a crown of
sharp, nasty thorns. If I remember correctly, he supposedly died
for the sins of mankind, and if we believe in Him as the Son of
God, and if we're truly repentant for the horrible things we've
done, we can be forgiven. We can be free of our guilt and suffering, our sense of hopelessness and self-loathing. That sounded to
me then as it does now like an excellent deal, because it's for damn
sure I needed forgiving, and it's for damn sure I couldn't get sober
if I couldn't forgive others.

Forgive myself?

I'm trying but it's a tough endeavor, one I'm certain never to
complete.

When I think of my brother, and I think of him every day, I
used to see him in bed, recoiling from the blast, the pillow darkening, growing heavy with blood. When I think of my sister, and
I think of her every day, I used to see her sprawled out on the
concrete banks of the Los Angeles River, her limbs bent in all the
wrong directions.

Those images are permanently etched in my mind.

But do they have to be the first and only things I remember about them? In forever lamenting the dead I am denying the lives of the living. I am robbing all those I love and hold most dear because I am preoccupied with the past and cannot fully give of myself in the present. In residing in the darkness, in fixating on the tragic, I am also robbing myself of the ability to remember my brother and sister in better times. They are more than alcoholics, and I dishonor them and all they mean to me by distilling their lives into their last moments of blinding pain. I dishonor them and myself by living in misery and mourning. Barry and Marilyn loved me as I loved them, and they would not have wanted me to forget that. I'm sure of it.

I am my own problem.

I am my own worst enemy.

I need to learn how to better reflect on my life. I need to learn how my behavior affects others. I need to learn how to care. I need to learn how to be kind and compassionate and quit judging everyone, including myself, and that's where A.A. comes in, and in more ways than in drinking. Be honest, it teaches. Treat others as you would like to be treated. Don't lie, cheat, or steal. Be respectful.

Show a little humility.

Living with the guilt and self-hatred caused by my drinking and using, and then trying for the better part of my life to drown out these feelings by drinking and using even more, played as much if not a larger role in destroying me than the booze and drugs ever did. Absolutely, they're a huge part of the problem, but equally important to this cycle of self-annihilation, if not more so, is my lack of spirituality.

That's the question I have for Nick when I call him the morning after I caught myself praying to the God I renounced when I was a kid, just seven, shaking my fist at the sky and cursing Him, waiting for a bolt of lightning to strike me dead.

"You think it's okay?" I ask.

"To pray to Jesus?"

"Yeah."

"Why wouldn't it be?"

"Because I'm a hypocrite," I say. "You know my story. I spent my entire life believing He didn't exist and now here I am asking for His help."

"I don't see the problem. But if you think it's a problem, apologize. Tell Him you changed your mind. What's the big deal?"

"So He's just supposed to let it go?"

"Yeah," Nick says. "If you tell Him you're sorry, and you mean it, it's His job to let you slide. Get yourself a Bible and start reading. Might want to try a little church, too, if you want to go the Christian route."

Church? That's taking it a step too far, and I tell him so.

"I go," he tells me. "Not all the time. But I go. I'm Catholic."

I figured Nick for a lot of things but never a Catholic. Catholics are right up there with Baptists, Mormons, and Jehovah's Witnesses, and there I go again. Judging.

"You never told me that," I say.

"You never asked," he says, "and it's not my place to tell you what to put your faith in. But in case you don't know it, A.A. was formed by evangelical Christians. That pisses off a lot of people, but the word *Father* and *Creator* are used I don't know how many times in the Big Book. And the Serenity Prayer, you know the one we always use at the end of a meeting?"

"Yeah?"

"Google it."

"What for?"

"Check out the second stanza, the one we *don't* say. It's about Jesus. It's a Christian prayer, man. The whole program is based on biblical principles. But keep that to yourself or you'll make a lot of enemies in A.A. The idea is to include everybody. Buddhists. Jews. Hindus. Muslims. Even atheists, like yourself, although they usually flip after a while. The only requirement," he says, "is a desire to stop drinking. The God thing is all on you."

This begins my *personal* journey back in time with memories of my sister leading the way. I stress the world *personal* because that's what faith is to a Christian, a one-on-one relationship with Jesus, though the Bible preaches that you have to go through the Father to get to the Son. You don't need to go to church, either, but I give it a shot, as Nick suggests. Where as a child I found the experience excruciatingly boring, now I'm only slightly bored, and it's not with the sermons but the hymns. I don't like singing. Never have. Never will. I choose the Lutheran brand in memory of my sister, and I drag my youngest son, Nate, with me (the last left in the nest) as my sister dragged me to church, if only to give him some exposure to the concept of God, just in case, later in life, he finds himself in a spot like me and needs the sort of help that no human, not even the most loving parent, can give him. I also choose the Lutheran brand because in addition to wading through the Bible, I read up on Martin Luther, and I come to admire his bravery, the intensity of his faith and thoughts on God, and how he took his life in his hands standing up for his beliefs against one of the most prominent, corrupt Western religions of his day. To further advance Nate's and my own terribly limited theological education, our pastor generously gives of his time, taking us through a series of private hour-long lessons about Lutheranism, God, faith, and the Holy Trinity. And when the last lesson is completed, my son and I get a full-emersion dunking in the chilly waters of Lake Arrowhead in the name of the Father, the Son, and the Holy Spirit.

If you ask my boy about it, he'll say he only got wet. If you ask me, it's about transformation, identification, and joining the ranks of others who believe. But it's also about the resurrection, and, by extension, my own, free of the alcoholic life of darkness and despair, suffering and guilt. The slate is wiped clean and I get to start over again.

And if I want to be forgiven, I must also learn to forgive others, and that includes, finally, my brother and sister. Anger and resentment are at the core of the gruesome images I hold of Barry and Marilyn, how they abandoned and betrayed me, how in attempting to relieve their suffering they inflicted me with my own, the kind I do my best to keep to myself. In forgiveness, however, is liberation, and I'm granted a choice. When I say to myself, yes, they are dead and I can't change that, I have to let them be, I have to let them rest; when I say they are free I am freeing myself, and they suddenly spring back to life in a much different way. Now, instead of images of suicide immediately popping into my head, I see Marilyn and myself, just kids, picking dandelions in MacArthur Park, not the yellow ones but the kind with furry white petals.

"Make a wish," she says, and I do, and together we blow on it and watch the particles float away in the wind. She smiles, and it's a beautiful smile. I see my brother's smile, too, a devilish one, and I remember him, the bastard, pinning me to the floor in one of the many apartments we lived in, letting a strand of spit slide between his lips, dangling over my face. The strand grows longer and longer and just before it falls he sucks it back into his mouth and laughs. Of course he doesn't always make it. And what about the time I catch Marilyn and her boyfriend making out on the couch, his hand under her blouse, and that look of shock on her face when I walk in on them? She's only fourteen. Or the time, years later, when Marilyn and I go to the premiere of *Bad Company* at a theater in Westwood, Barry's name plastered on the marquee along with Jeff Bridges's? It's Barry's first starring role in a movie, his first big break, and I'm proud of him. My big brother. I'm still proud. That is also the first time I ever wore a tie. Marilyn made me.

For each minute spent remembering the sadness of their lives, I subtract one from my own, and without sobriety I most certainly would never have understood the high cost of this loss. Just the other day, I picked a dandelion from the forest, thought of Marilyn, and made a wish. She's with me. She's smiling. We blow on it together and I feel her breath on the side of my cheek, just barely, like a soft kiss.

The furry white petals disappear into the sky.

So it is that I begin as an atheist at the ripe old age of seven, begrudgingly find myself in A.A. in my forties, and because of A.A. ultimately end up one of those reborns that most of my friends who don't have a drinking or drug problem like to joke about. A few not-so-close friends even despise me for it.

But so what?

So what if when I reach the end of the line and there is no God, that in fact it's all a Great Big Nothing, will I have wasted my last years attempting to live a sober life of dignity and respect and remembering the dead with love and warmth instead of regret and heartache? Is it right or wrong to believe in something you don't know for sure even exists? That you can't see or touch? Will I, in the end, be considered a fool because of it? I think I know the answer, my own answer anyway, but I can't seem to find it in words.

This Little Boy

This little boy lives in the apartment across from mine. His hair is blond. His eyelashes are so light as to be almost invisible in the sun. He is underfed and thin and his button-down shirt is too small for him. His jeans are some off brand picked from the bargain bin at Sears or J. C. Penney or the racks of the Salvation Army. Only the poorest of us wear anything but Levi's, and he is among them, this little boy. I'm six years old and he's maybe seven or eight. One front tooth overlaps the other and the bottom row is crowded together.

We don't know each other. I never knew his name. He is a child, like me, growing up in a cheap apartment complex in East San Jose. I sometimes tell myself that I have no reason to remember him, and yet here I am, sixty years old, still thinking about this little boy. I sometimes tell myself that I made him up, that he's another character in some story I started a long time ago and never finished. But he's not. He's real, and if I were to write a story about him tomorrow, I'd change it up, so he wouldn't be skinny because there was no food in the cupboards. I'll make sure he always has some mac and cheese on hand and plenty of peanut butter and jelly. Milk, certainly there will be milk in the refrigerator, and eggs, and bread, there's no reason not to have a loaf of bread around. These things are cheap enough, and if for whatever reason he *does* have to go hungry, as children in America sometimes do, it won't be for more than a day or two, and never because his mother is a negligent alcoholic. If they're down on their luck, it'll be because she lost her job, but she's looking hard for another, not sitting around all day drinking wine from a box.

But this is precisely how I remember her, a middle-aged woman with thin, tight lips sitting on a beat-up sofa chair on her apartment balcony. On a small table rests the box of wine, and nearly every day when I come home from school, or on warm summer nights when I step out onto my own apartment balcony, there she is on hers across the way, drinking that cheap wine, chain-smoking and flipping through the glossy pages of some gossip magazine. Of course at my age I don't yet know what an alcoholic is. All I think is that she is lazy. Now I believe that she is both, because I've since learned how quickly alcohol can turn on you, make you mean where it once made you happy, and how that meanness left unchecked can sicken the soul and the mind. But I also don't believe in excuses. Certain acts, regardless of circumstance, are beyond justification.

In my story I won't hear the boy scream through the thin apartment walls. There won't be any late-night scenes where my father climbs out of bed and puts on his bathrobe and slippers and goes to their apartment. She never opens the door but the screaming always stops, usually subsiding into sobs before it's quiet again. And when a woman in a pantsuit, a man in a dress coat, and a police officer come to the apartment one day and take the boy away, it'll have nothing to do with alcoholism and the cruelty that often accompanies it.

In my story the authorities are making a mistake. She's really a good mother who loves her child and those marks on his arms and legs and back are from falling off his bicycle. Or getting into fights. This boy is no scrapper. He's weak and scrawny with crooked teeth and his skin is white in a mostly brown and black neighborhood. Of course he's going to get a little banged up. If it's a teacher who reports him to the authorities, she has it all wrong.

He's gone for about a month.

It's not how long he's gone that gets me, though, so much as how far he must've had to walk. I'm sure they didn't place him in a foster home down the street or around the block. This little boy embarks on a serious journey. Imagine a seven- or eight-year-old navigating miles and miles of twists and turns of suburban neighborhoods and city streets. Imagine him crossing a busy intersection during rush hour. And how can he remember the way home? Does he have a map? Can he even read one at his age? I'm sure he gets lost. Undoubtedly he has to backtrack more than once and ask strangers for directions. It's exhausting, too, his legs ache, his feet throb, and as the day slips into night fear sets in.

So maybe this kid is no scrapper but that doesn't mean he isn't tough inside. I respect his grit and determination. His resolve. His devotion and tenacity. It's something primal that drives him.

That's how I'd write it, anyway, the story of a boy unjustly wrenched from the arms of his loving mother by heartless authorities, but ultimately, against all odds, child and parent are reunited.

It's right against wrong.

Good versus evil.

Late at night, after a grueling journey, this boy finally arrives at the doorstep of his apartment. His mother pulls him to her bosom and holds him tightly, as he longs to be held, and the cries I hear through the thin walls of my bedroom are ones of joy. The tears are from happiness, not agony, so the part where that same night she burns holes in his arm with a cigarette doesn't belong in my story. I need to create a different truth. I need to revise. I need to make it mine when in fact I can do no such thing.

But I can lie.

I can make this a place where there is no human cruelty. In my story I can reinvent the boy I cannot forget and remember him not for the pain and suffering he endured but for the haunting power of a child's love for the parent, no matter how perilous that love may be.

Seasons

He has his last check sent to my home address. It's from the Montana Department of Corrections in the amount of $401.63. Maybe I shouldn't have opened the envelope, but I thought it might've had something to do with the letter I'd drafted on his behalf for his parole hearing. I wrote it on university letterhead to try to impress the board members. Whether it helped or not, I do not know, but I'm told that he's free now and his check is still here. I'm sure he needs the money. I know he'll call. I just don't know when. It's been a month, and I've begun to worry.

I hope that all the letters we write each other while he's in prison make some kind of difference. But I had also hoped that all the hours we spent talking and poring over the Big Book at Bill's Diner would have made some kind of difference and they ultimately did not. We talk as many hours on the phone. We work on the Steps meticulously, laboriously, and we attend meetings together three times a week. Often I pick him up at his mother's house, and he seems happy. He seems committed to living a clean and sober life. I know he is proud of himself the night he claims his first-year chip, and I am proud for him. His mother, a re-covering alcoholic-addict herself, gives him his cake in front of a packed room, and she is proud, too, and crying. I know there are some there who never thought he would get this far, but he proves them wrong.

I'll call him Ty, though that is not his real name, and he bucks the odds for ex-felons and lands a good-paying construction job. He gets his driver's license back after having it revoked years be-fore and buys a lowered Honda. And the girls, he soon has plenty of girlfriends, because he's handsome and charming, and they seem drawn to that bad-boy reputation. I caution him not to play one against the other, to get one girl's hopes up and dash an-other's. Deceit is endemic to our old lifestyle and we can't go there anymore. Hurting women is degrading, and in degrading them, we are, in effect, degrading ourselves. That's a tough one for Ty, and I know he hears my admonitions, I warn him many times, but I don't believe he ever really listens. I personally know this lie all too well, having cheated on my first wife, and now, sober, finally realizing how selfish and devastatingly hurtful duplicity is.

I won't tell him that he let me down because this isn't and never has been about me. But I think it's fair to say that Ty gives up on himself. I also think it's fair to say that someone who's spent nearly ten of his twenty-eight years in juvenile hall and prison has a skewed vision of himself and that it makes him more susceptible to giving up and returning to the criminal mind-set he knows best.

For Ty, the life of chaos and turmoil begins early, being thrown into foster care at the age of nine when the courts de-termine that his parents are unfit to raise him. Then, when they clean up, he's allowed to return home for a year before his parents start using again and the insanity overwhelms them, as it does Ty, because this time around he discovers their stash of meth and helps himself to a sample. Nothing, before or since, has ever made him feel better than the rush of that first blast, but then his parents are busted again, and he's right back where he left off, in foster care. And it's not as if these foster homes in the backwoods or small towns of Montana, or anywhere for that matter, necessarily have a child's best interests at heart. A kid like Ty gets bounced around from place to place as if they're more trouble than they're worth, and since he's using meth now whenever he can get his hands on it, and since the government checks for his care don't amount to much, he finds himself on a whirlwind tour of the state of Montana, until, maybe inevitably, he winds up most at home in youth detention centers for stealing and robbing to feed his growing habit. How is he supposed to learn about love and kindness, right and wrong, good from bad, when his friends and family apparently don't know much about these things, either? Or, if they do, is it possible that they're simply too high, stoned, or drunk to share them? At some point these questions become an irrelevancy and fade into the background of his life. The drugs turn into their own problem independent of one's past.

Despite all the adversity and hardship, I advise him to stop blaming others for his own troubles. I advise him to forgive his father. I advise him to forgive his mother. I know she feels intense guilt for abandoning him, but she leaves the man who batters her, moves to California, and turns her life around. She works her way through college, remarries, and becomes a registered nurse, and now she allows Ty, a grown man, to live in her home. And she is, after all, the reason he and I know each other. She is, after all, the person who introduces us at a meeting, and how, when I invite Ty for a cup of coffee later that night, he asks me to sponsor him. More important, however, is that issue of forgiveness. He's no safer harboring resentments than I am. In the poor schools I attend growing up, I take beatings from black and brown students because of my white skin, but it hardly compares to the vicious attacks he suffers in prison. I've never had to choose sides according to race to survive, and I've long since learned to move beyond my prejudices and anger and make all sorts of friends without regard to color or sexual orientation. Does he remember we worked on this? Does he remember how I repeatedly tell him that he can't allow himself to see the black and brown faces of those who hurt him in all the black and brown people who have not? That hate begets hate. This is a hard lesson for him, because he prides himself as a fighter who knows to strike before being struck, who knows that the first one stunned is most likely the first one to hit the ground, and it's on the ground when others join in, swarming.

I get that.

I also get that being a so-called man in prison is about respect and dignity. Inmates are stripped of these things, and in their place emerges a warped sense of masculinity. What passes for honor is in truth largely fear, and if someone brushes shoulders with Ty when he's walking the halls, or looks at him the wrong way, that's reason to fight or worse. But outside those walls it's a different world, and respect is about control. About treating others as he would like to be treated. It is not earned through violence but rather by turning away from it whenever possible, by being responsible, calm, and collected instead of exploding and striking out. We boil it down to a simple phrase, a mantra that I ask him to repeat every time he feels the rage building inside him, regardless of the cause or rationale: *Lose your cool, go back to prison . . . lose your cool, go back to prison.* Even he admits that this small suggestion makes a significant difference when one night six months into his sobriety he stops at a Burger King in San Bernardino and the kid working the drive-through gives him change for a ten instead of the twenty he hands him. Rather than consider the possibility that it's an innocent mistake, he immediately thinks the worst, that the kid is trying to cheat him, and Ty calls him on it. He insists he's right. The kid insists he's wrong, and instead of letting it go at that, Ty parks his car, gets out, and tries to go inside. But it's late and the doors are locked. Only the drive-through is open, and yet he is about to pound on the glass doors and start hollering, demanding his money, before it dawns on him that if the cops come they'll surely take the word of the kid in a paper hat over an adult ex-con on felony probation for grand theft auto and possession of narcotics.

"I heard your voice, man," he tells me, "and I said fuck it and got back in my car. Shit, I didn't even wait for my burger and fries."

I praise him.

I tell him that's progress. I tell him that he did the right and smart thing. That he can't afford to lose his temper anymore. That he has to relearn how to live peacefully and that means letting go of his hate and resentment toward blacks and browns and cops and prison guards and gays and lesbians and kids working at the Burger King, and, yes, even the molester in our group who's on the Megan's Law list for lewd or lascivious acts with a child under fourteen years of age. This guy did his time, too, and we're supposed to help even the most wretched among us, including white supremacists, when the mutual goal is sobriety. I work with Ty because he needs the guidance of a clean and sober older man who's battled anger and addiction much longer than he has.

Ty graduates from the youth detention centers to the state prison one night while he's walking the streets in downtown Billings, Montana, and comes across a Corvette. It's parked in the driveway of a car dealership, and it's idling, keys in the ignition. He looks around but doesn't see anyone. To hear him tell it, it's the owner's fault. Only a fool would leave an extraordinarily fast and expensive sports car alone with the motor running and not expect an eighteen-year-old kid strung out on methamphetamine to slip behind the wheel and take it for a ride. Since he plans to return it after a couple laps around the block, maybe a quick drive through town, he sees no harm in his actions. The owner won't even have time to report it stolen before he has it back. That he's already on probation for misdemeanor petty theft, a crime he says he didn't commit, apparently doesn't cross his mind, not when he's high, anyway, and feeling down over his girlfriend breaking up with him just hours before. It's why he's walking the streets at night in the first place, trying to figure shit out, what he said to her, where he went wrong, and the last thing he's thinking about is how a little joyride might make his situation all the worse, assuming he's caught, though he's sure that he won't be. Besides, fuck the law. Fuck cops. He keeps seeing the sweaty face of that black pig who threw him facedown on the hood of the cruiser and cuffed him on the petty theft charge outside Wal-Mart for stealing a bicycle, which he swears he didn't do. He tells me what he tells the cop. That somebody gave him the bike. He says he had no idea it was stolen. He tells me he can't walk the streets without the pigs shaking him down every time they lay eyes on him. "That's fucked up, man," is how he puts it. "You feel me? You feel me?" These are phrases he uses often, and no, I don't *feel* him, but I'll nod and agree as he lays out his story for me, because as his sponsor I need to gain his trust before I can help him, assuming I can, and I'm not so sure about that. His problems, like my own, run deeper than drugs and alcohol, though without sobriety he can't even begin to address them.

However troubled Ty's past, I'm not buying that even a drug-addled eighteen-year-old, especially one on probation, doesn't have the ability to assess the wisdom of jumping behind the wheel of a Corvette, gunning the engine, and tearing off down the street. Something else is at work here. And I think I understand it from the homes and office buildings I burglarized when I was a teenager. I'm not proud of what I did. It was wrong. It was bad. I knew it then and I know it now. But breaking and entering and the excitement of what you might find, of what you might get—guns, cash, jewelry, it's always a surprise—coupled with the risk of getting shot or caught by the cops is a tremendous adrenaline rush, a huge thrill, a real kick. So a part of me is with him when he hits the gas and he's thrust back in his seat, the road ahead disappearing beneath him, the lampposts and buildings blurring to the sides. Another part, the sober adult, feels shame and guilt for identifying with Ty. The compulsion for crime is a compulsion akin to addiction.

He's excited, animated, gesturing as he tells me about the Corvette at Bill's Diner where I also meet regularly with my own sponsor who is slowly wasting away from cancer as Ty and I talk. I shake my head, more in resignation than disapproval, because I know that there's only one way this story can end. Of course he gets lit up by the Billings police, and of course because he's young and stupid and whacked out on meth, instead of pulling over he leads them on a high-speed chase through town and onto the interstate and soon enough crashes the Corvette into a telephone pole. He doesn't hurt anyone but himself, breaking his leg and shattering his kneecap, which will leave him with a slight limp for the rest of his life.

"It was fucking wild," he says, and he says it gleefully, as if it's something to be proud of. I would prefer that he feel regret for his actions, as I came to feel for my crimes as a teenager, and I tell him that it was not fucking wild. It was fucking stupid. His smile fades, as it should, and he could've left then. He could've gotten up and walked out of the diner but he chose to stay.

I'm glad he does.

Maybe he's ready to listen to the old dog and stop romanticizing crime and rationalizing irrational drugged-out behavior. This one impulsive act turns a violation of probation on a misdemeanor petty theft charge from a six-month sentence in the county jail to a years-long stint at Montana State Prison for grand theft auto, possession of narcotics, evading arrest, and a host of other serious tack-on charges. And Ty is lucky it isn't worse. The district attorney pleads a twelve-year sentence down to eight, and somehow, though his behavior in prison is far from model, he's out in six. If he violates the conditions of his parole, however, if he tests dirty, and his parole officer tests him monthly, it's back to Montana to serve out the remainder of his eight-year sentence. For Ty the cost of getting high is the difference between living free or wasting life locked up.

In some ways, he knows how to function better in prison than in the complicated world outside of it. The longer you're in, I'm told, the harder it is to stay out. I ask Ty the question I ask of two other ex-cons I've sponsored, one of whom is back in prison, the other last spotted by another A.A. member a few months earlier on the streets of San Bernardino, apparently using again. I have also asked this same question of a group of prisoners I visited for an A.A. meeting, and I do it, as I do with Ty, to shed light on the obvious.

"These crimes," I say, "how many did you do when you were high?"

"Just the ones I got caught for?"

"All of them," I say.

"Fuck, I did a lot of stuff, man. I can't even remember it all."

"Were you high? That's all I'm asking."

He shrugs. "Yeah, mostly. Either high or coming down. Jonesing, you know."

"You see what I'm saying," I say.

"What?"

"We fuck up when we get loaded. We do stuff we wouldn't ordinarily do. Like steal Corvettes. Or hurt or rob people. I bet you wouldn't have done half the shit you did if you weren't high." Ty is drinking a Coke, and he looks away, begins fidgeting with the straw. "Something has to change," I say, "and that something is you."

I'd told him to bring a pen and a notebook to our meeting, and now I ask him to get out that pen. Open that notebook. He's quick to the task, and as he fumbles to open the notebook I detect enthusiasm in his eyes, a hint of eagerness, and his spirit buoys my own. He likes that I have a plan. I don't tell him that it's just basic A.A. protocol with a little extra due diligence thrown in for protection.

"Here's what you're going to do," I say. "You ready? I want you to write this down."

The list begins with having him call me every night between seven and nine, followed by daily readings in the Big Book, beginning with "The Doctor's Opinion," which I tell him I'll quiz him on the next time we meet, here at Bill's this coming Friday night before the meeting. I want him to pray every morning and ask God, whoever or whatever his God may be, to keep him sober today. I want him to pray every night and thank God, whoever or whatever his God may be, for keeping him sober today and ask that He do the same for him tomorrow. I want him to meditate when he wakes up. Just sit on the floor and be still and quiet and try to stop your thoughts from racing before you reach for that first cup of coffee. Begin with a minute or two and work up to ten. We'll start with Step One and get to the Fourth and Fifth as soon as we can. These Steps made the greatest difference for me. When I did them with my sponsor, I tell him, I felt, for the first time in my decades-long struggle to get clean and sober, *safe* from the desire to pick up a drink or a drug.

No matter how meticulously we follow the same path, no one, including myself, can guarantee we'll get the same results, but it's more than worth a shot, and so this is how we begin. And we stick to it. And he does well, he does wonderfully until one night, a few weeks after earning his first-year chip, he goes to a party in San Bernardino where everyone is drinking and having a great time. Why can't he enjoy himself, too? Couple that reasoning with the bright idea that his problem is and always has been with meth, not booze, and he's free to have a beer or two. Or three. Regrettably he doesn't call to share his bright idea with me before he cracks open that first beer, suspecting, I imagine, that I wouldn't find it all that bright. Though alcohol may never have been a problem for Ty, I would've told him that it'll make him vulnerable, that it'll lower his resistance, and that soon enough he'll return to his drug of choice.

But if alcohol isn't a problem, why does he drive up the mountain drunk and crash his lowered Honda into a tree as he's trying to maneuver the turn onto his mother's street? It's four in the morning, there are few cars on the road and no sheriffs around, and because he's lucky and isn't badly injured, he leaves the Honda, which is totaled, and walks home. It's demoralizing and humiliating to confess to his mother that he messed up, but he's her son, she loves him, and so she covers for him, reporting the collision to the sheriff's department and the insurance company and telling them it was her fault, that she had been driving. A DUI is no small violation of Ty's parole, and if not for his mother he could've ended up serving out the last two of his eight-year sentence at Montana State.

The next day, he calls me.

He says he slipped, that he screwed up, he needs to talk. We meet and he gives me the sordid details while hanging his head, unable to look me in the eyes. For having been in a crash, he fares well, incurring only a deep laceration under his chin, patched with

butterfly bandages, and an oblong lump on his forehead that's beginning to turn black and yellow around the edges.

He thinks he let me down when really he has only let himself
down. He expects me to be outraged, to raise my voice in anger and reprimand him, like a child, but I do no such thing. I've
relapsed myself more times than I can remember, and my own
sponsor, when he learns that he has terminal cancer, retreats to
the bottle after fifteen years of sobriety. But he's sober again now.
That's what matters. That Ty is here. That he's already back on
track by meeting with me. All this is not to say that relapsing is
no big deal. It is. But he can also learn from it, taking stock of the
triggers that led to that first drink, and hereafter being vigilant
of them.

Surprisingly, at least to Ty, I am neither shocked nor incensed.
We beat up enough on ourselves when we screw up and don't
need anyone else beating on us, too. I suggest we get back to work
right away, start over on the Steps, and do a more thorough inventory on the Fourth. Each time we relapse, there's new stuff to
add to the list, and also typically a few things we likely forgot to
include the first time around. We part with Ty feeling a little better about himself, knowing that he's not alone in relapsing, that
sadly it's more the norm than the exception with people like us.
But that doesn't relieve him from taking responsibility. I tell him
that there may not be a next time. That he could die, like so many
others who slip. Does he want to take that chance?

Is it worth it?

He knows the answer.

So what happens that very day between the time we talk and
a few hours later, at 6:45 p.m., when I come to pick him up at his

mother's house to take him to a meeting and he's not there? She's not home, either. I call his cell but it goes to voicemail. I leave a message, telling him to call me. He doesn't. Days pass. I call once more. Once more it goes to voicemail. I suspect the worst, and my suspicions are confirmed when I see his mother at a meeting later that week. Ty got into a fight with his stepfather that afternoon, who is also a recovering alcoholic-addict, but an unforgiving one, and because Ty slipped, because he had his mother assume blame for crashing the car, his stepfather kicks him out of the house. I'm sure it's an ugly scene, and I empathize with Ty's situation, being thrown out with nowhere to go when he already feels rotten about himself, but that's not an excuse to implode. That's how we need to think, anyway, but the truth is that we each have our own breaking point where we feel compelled to shut out the world and all our thoughts and emotions and retreat to the place that brings us comfort from our pain, confusion, and anger. But does the drink or drug really offer relief? And, if so, how long does it last before life spins out of control again? The thing is, it's all inside the head, and you can't escape yourself. I've tried and tried and it's never worked.

Ty is now something of a ghost. An enigma. Gossip abounds within the A.A. circle. One week someone spots him at the 7-Eleven in the neighboring town of Crestline. Another week he's seen walking into the forest with a paper bag under his arm. His boss says he hasn't been to work in a month but that someone broke into a shed at their construction site and stole a thousand dollars' worth of power tools. He's not saying it's Ty, but Ty knew those tools were there.

Nearly a year passes before Ty is arrested at a storage unit

in Skyforest with another tweaker, a girl, a sixteen-year-old runaway. Apparently the two of them had been living there, and
inside the unit, among his dirty clothing and hers, the sheriff
finds all sorts of stolen goods, from TVs to microwaves, which
explains the rash of home burglaries reported in the crime log
of the *Mountain News*. They also find a quarter ounce of meth,
pipes and syringes, and a triple-beam scale for weighing drugs for
sales. Ty is fucked. The paper prints his mug shot, looking drawn
and wasted, his eyes sunken, his cheeks sucked in. The girl is a
minor and escapes the public humiliation of a photo, or even the
mention of her name. It's another six months before I finally hear
from him again.

It's one of those automated calls from the West Valley Detention Center in Rancho Cucamonga, asking if I'll accept a collect
call from an inmate. I think we have a time limit of fifteen minutes, but we don't use more than five. All he wants is for me to
visit him. Except for his mother, nobody has come to see him, no
friends, no one from our A.A. group, not even the sister I never
knew he had. This troubles me. Shouldn't his sister have been part
of his Fourth Step inventory? I find it hard to believe that there's
been no emotional injury, no bad blood between the two of them,
which makes me wonder what else Ty didn't tell me about and
why. On a personal level I could not care less about the specif-
ics, but the honesty part, coming clean with our resentments and
those we've harmed, intentionally or not, that there's no getting
around.

In jail he's well-fed and looks nothing like his mug shot. It's
amazing how quickly he rebounds, but then he is young. Thirty
now? Thirty-one? A sheet of plexiglass separates us and we sit on

hard plastic chairs and talk into old-fashioned phone receivers. He's dressed in orange prison scrubs, and he tells me his "cellie is cool, down with the brothers," and he does not mean blacks or browns. Smiling, he stands and pulls up his shirt, showing me his latest tat, the word *peckerwood* inked across his chest in large, Old English–style lettering. Am I supposed to be impressed? Is he showing me this in defiance of everything we talked about, that we tried to change and move beyond? Ty brags about how he "fucked up a nigger, a big motherfucker, too," on the bus from the holding tank in San Bernardino to this place when the guy ordered him to "get up, white boys in the back." I don't know what to say. I don't know what to advise. If the visitors in the lobby are any indication, his color and kind are vastly outnumbered here, and maybe he needs to be this way again, full of hate and hostility, prison imperatives for staying alive. I wish he could once and for all clean up and do his time and learn from his mistakes and not waste the rest of his life killing whatever good could come of it. "There's no iron in the yards here. They took the weights away in California, and you're all buff and shit, man. Can you put together a workout for me, something I can do in my cell?" I tell him I will. We're given one automated warning two minutes before the line allowing us to speak between the thick glass goes dead, and he nods goodbye to me as I stand. I nod back, anxious to get out of here, to put this day, this memory behind me.

The courts are overloaded with cases and apparently it's too much trouble to try him for burglary and the lesser offense of harboring and contributing to the delinquency of a runaway minor. Apparently it's too much trouble to try him at all and his public defender strikes a deal with the district attorney. Ty serves two

years for possession of narcotics and stolen goods in California
and then he's transferred back to Montana to finish up the last
two of his previous eight-year sentence. Even though he loses another four years of his life to prison, which is exactly where he
belongs, it's still a gravy deal. Why I answer his letters, however,
I do not know. Maybe I feel sorry for him. If that's the reason,
there is no rational basis for it. He knows where drugs took him
before and they have taken him there again. He admits as much
in his letters, heavily laced with remorse and sorrow, but at least
he is clean now, they have A.A. in prison, and he says he attends
every meeting they allow him. He says he's reading the Big Book
again, and the Bible, too, and praying. Lots of praying. I respond
to his letters with encouragement, urging him to stay out of trouble, to try not to get into fights, and every few months I put a little
money into his account for snacks and toiletries. Ty promises to
pay me back but I don't expect or want it. These are not loans.
He asks for a subscription to *Maxim* and I get it for him. It's the
closest thing to pornography the prison allows, and it's hardly
pornography with women in lingerie and bikinis.

The Montana Department of Corrections may not in truth
correct anything, other than what might be exacted through the
punishment of incarceration, but they do understand the importance of money for a convict's survival when he's returned to the
community. However meager the pay, they give him a job in the
mess hall eighteen months prior to his release. In that time he saves
two thousand dollars, not including his last check of $401.63, but
as a former dope dealer he's used to keeping his cash in hand.
Maybe he never learned to open a bank account. Maybe it never
occurs to him that his money would be safer in a bank than a

hiding spot at his father's place in the woods on the outskirts of Billings. He lets Ty stay with him for a few weeks until he can get permission from his parole officer to move back to California. It sounds too incredible. It sounds so ill-fated, so disastrous that my first thought, when his mother tells me about it, is that it's a lie. But she shows me her cell phone. She shows me the picture Ty sent her of the house reduced to ashes, and all his cash, of course, up in smoke with it. The only thing left standing is the stone chimney, and in the background is a skinny little boy, shirtless, poking through the rubble with a stick. I have no idea who he is. A relative? A curious neighbor kid? Assuming Ty stays clean while he's locked up, it's possible that losing all his hard-earned seed money sets him off again. It doesn't have to be that way, though. He could turn the situation around and be grateful that no one is in the house when it catches fire and burns to the ground. He could consider that he narrowly escaped a horribly painful death.

He's *alive*.

Terrible as it is to lose all that money, especially for an ex-con who needs every cent of it to get back on his feet, it is still only that, money, and he can make more. Awful things happen all the time, and he can use them as a way of strengthening his resolve to stay sober rather than letting it take him down, like that house, in a blaze of fire and ash. I know that looking at it this way is easier said than done, and when I learn that he's back in California, living on the mountain again but I don't hear from him right away, I begin to doubt. I begin to worry. I want to think that he's fine, that nobody fresh out of prison after all those years would immediately return to the drug that put him there.

Of all people, however, I should know better.

Cell phone reception in mountainous terrain is poor. When he finally does call, his voice cuts in and out, but despite the intermittent static we manage to communicate. But it's all business. Nothing congratulatory. No excitement over his release. Nothing about how wonderful it must feel to be free again. I want to chalk up his lack of enthusiasm to the urgency of a bad connection, the need to say only what needs to be said before we lose each other again, but there's something off, something nervous and hurried in his voice, and we talk no longer than it takes to arrange a time to meet for him to pick up his last check. I assume he lost all his belongings in the fire, so after we hang up I rummage through my closet and dresser drawers for some clothes for him. I hesitate to part with one of my favorite jackets, but it's November, winter is near, and he'll need a good jacket. We're about the same size, and it's leather, black leather, with a heavy wool lining.

The following afternoon I pick him up outside the 7-Eleven in Crestline. He's leaning against the pay phone when I arrive. As he approaches my car, I can tell he's lost weight, and when he climbs inside, he doesn't look me in the eye. His hand, when we shake, feels sweaty and clammy, and I know immediately that he's high. "I dig your new wheels," he says. I'm driving a black BMW, and it unexpectedly becomes a measure of just how long he's been away, because I've owned this car for several years. "Bet this fucker's fast, huh?" He is right about that, and the idea of a car sends a signal to his brain. "I was going to buy a car. You can't get a job without a car. I guess my mom told you about the fire. What fucking luck. Two thousand bucks. Poof. Gone. Can you believe that shit?" He talks fast, running his sentences together, and then he's quiet, as if he suddenly realizes that he's given himself away, that I know he's tweaking, and his shame is palpable. But there's no need for that. I want to tell him to relax. I already figured he was high when he called the other day and he confirmed it the second he climbed into my car and lowered his eyes.

On the way to my bank he continually pinches at the knee of his jeans, rolling the fabric between his fingers, releasing it, then pinching at it again. The teller, a middle-aged woman with a British accent, has seen his type before. There are plenty like him on the mountain and she is justifiably suspicious of cashing his check. He is used to it, being looked down on for the sagging jeans he wears, the oversized T-shirt, the blue knit cap pulled down over his ears. It's the uniform of estrangement. At one time I aroused similar mistrust, not so much for my dress as that sunken, gaunt dead-giveaway look of your common junkie, of your common drunk, but I am a respectable man now. I am healthy. I have reclaimed my life, and this teller has never met that other man. She only knows who I am today, a professor with enough in my account to cover Ty's otherwise worthless endorsement of his own check. I can see the disapproval on her face. What am I doing with this drug addict, cashing this check from the Montana Department of Corrections? What terrible things did he do to wind up there? How is it that he came into my life? I don't judge or condemn her for it. Her reaction is a normal one for a person who does not associate with people like Ty and my former self. Despite outward appearances, he and I were once sadly in much the same position, and I have not forgotten who I once was and who I could very well become again. I have not forgotten about Ty, either, and I know that I am not supposed to give up hope on even the most hopeless among us, but he has worn me down. I have lost faith in him. He has traded one form of confinement for another, an even smaller cell, a prisoner locked up in his mind for the drugs he consumes.

The teller counts the cash out to me. I hand it to him as we leave the bank. I know it won't last long. He thanks me. He smiles, and I see his teeth, already blackening around the gums. Instead of shooting meth, he is smoking it now, or doing both, though I don't notice any tracks on his skinny arms. He must understand that when this little bit of money runs out and he can't get a job and he commits another serious crime and gets caught that it will be his third strike and he will be sentenced to twenty-five years to life without the possibility of parole.

"Where you staying?"

"Just drop me back off at the 7-Eleven," he says.

"You sure?"

"Yeah, I'm meeting a friend."

Some friend, I think.

His mother already told me that he's not living with her. His stepfather won't have him. The best I can figure is that wherever he's staying, he doesn't want me knowing about it, and I assume that's the way it will be from now on for us. I let him off where I picked him up in the parking lot of the 7-Eleven with a garbage bag full of clothes and a good heavy jacket that I didn't really want to part with. He'll be surprised when he opens the bag and finds it. I think he'll like it, and I hope it keeps him warm when the snow comes tonight. It's in the forecast. Already the clouds are rolling in and there is a sharp chill in the air and the wind is blowing and the leaves of the trees are falling to the ground. The light is draining from the sky. Snow will soon blanket the mountains and a quietness will descend upon the streets of this small town, leaving Ty adrift and abandoned, feeling very small and very lonely, lost in the darkness of his own making.

Bone by Bone

One quart of carrots. Two cups of beet juice. One cup each of cabbage and cauliflower and broccoli and a heaping teaspoon of turmeric. Throw it all into a high-powered juicer and flip the switch.

This is Nick's breakfast.

Lunch consists of lentils, peas, onions, garlic, leek, and chives and a sprinkling of whole-grain, gluten-free brown rice. Again the ingredients are mixed together, liquefied, and drunk. Dinner can be any variation of the aforementioned concoctions, but should also include either unsweetened applesauce, figs, dried apricots, or fresh pineapple.

Each Tuesday night, soon as my last class lets out, I race to pick up Nick for the Men's Stag. I race because I want to arrive early enough so that we have a little time to visit and talk before the meeting. These may be his last months. He might have longer. He might have less. Nobody, including his doctors, knows for sure, so these days are precious.

I'm willing to skip dinner until I get home later that evening, but Nick doesn't see the sense in it. "You're not doing me or your-self any favors going hungry. Eat," he says. "Eat. Order what you want." Usually we go to Bill's Diner where, as he sips on a cup of chamomile tea, I devour, in front of his very eyes, a cheeseburger and fries and wash it all down with a Diet Coke.

He is hoping against hope that the certified holistic nutri-tionist that he's hired can do for him what the doctors and chemo cannot.

"Cancer," he tells me, "thrives in acidity. And if I can just balance it out and raise my pH levels, it'll kill the cancer cells. Or at least slow the bastards down. That's the idea, anyway."

At this stage, any idea is a good idea. Any plan is better than no plan. Unfortunately, over the last couple of months, his liquid alkaline diet seems to be making him thinner and weaker instead of stronger and better. But I'm not about to say anything. What matters is right now. What matters is that he's sitting across from me. That we're together.

The waitress comes to our table and takes my plate. I've cleaned it. Not a morsel left, except for a soggy strand of lettuce.

"Was it good?" Nick asks.

"Yeah," I say.

"It looked good, especially for someone who had a broccoli smoothie for dinner."

It's our game. We play it every week, if not at Bill's Diner then Starbucks where I might order a donut or cinnamon roll to hold me over. Either way it's the same.

"I told you I don't have to eat in front of you. It's not like you weren't warned."

He brushes it off with a wave of his hand.

"No, I understand. I get it," he says. "You're just trying to help me out here. If I had a friend who couldn't eat any of the foods he loves, hamburgers, fried chicken, pizza, you name it, I'd scarf it down in front of him just like you. I wouldn't want him to forget what he's missing. That," he says, "*that* would be cruel."

"How about I order a big fat slice of cheesecake," I say. "That's your favorite, right? I'll eat it slow, too, just tiny little bits at a time. Draw it out, you know. Savor it. Make it last."

We go back and forth like this for a while and then shift gears and talk about boxing maybe, usually the neglected lighter weights, as the aficionados of boxing tend to do. Or the Red Sox. He's a huge fan and always wears a Boston Red Sox cap, even before the chemo, before he lost all his hair. Tonight I give him a hard time about the Allman Brothers T-shirt he's so fond of wearing lately. It has four toadstool mushrooms on the front. On the back it lists the dates they played at the Beacon Theatre in New York in 2012, a few months after Nick's diagnosis. The Allman Brothers are his favorite band, and as a kind of parting gift, a last hurrah, one of his brothers bought tickets for them. They flew out there and went to the concert and had a great time. I understand his brother somehow got a message to the stage manager and that the band, in Nick's honor, played his all-time favorite song of theirs, "Melissa."

I nod at the mushrooms on the T-shirt.

"Those are psilocybin, you know."

"Maybe."

"No maybes about it. Those are psilocybin. What kind of

message do you think that sends to the newcomers trying to get sober. Drinking is bad," I say, "but psychedelics? Hey, let's watch the walls melt."

"You can be a real asshole sometimes, you know that."

I have him going. No sense in stopping now.

"Too bad they didn't put a big marijuana leaf on there. Better yet, a syringe. You look like an old hippie in that shirt. I bet you're a Grateful Dead fan, too."

"Matter of fact, I am an old hippie." He takes off his Red Sox cap, showing his bald head. "Minus the hair." He scoffs. "The Grateful Dead? Jerry Garcia compared to Duane Allman on the guitar? Please. They're not even in the same league." He looks at his watch. "We better get going," he says. "The meeting starts in a half hour."

It's only a five-minute drive but Nick isn't moving so quickly these days. Getting in and out of my car is something of a chore. He's not so steady on his feet anymore, and he'd be smart to use a cane, but I can understand why he doesn't. I wouldn't want a cane, either. A cane means you're losing. At fifty-six he used to jog around the lake regularly, which is about a five-mile run. Now, at fifty-seven, walking down the flight of stairs from his house to the driveway to meet me on Tuesday nights winds him. Walking up them, when I drop him off, is much harder, and he has to stop several times along the way to rest and catch his breath. I'd help him, but I know he'd feel insulted if I asked, so instead I wait and watch from inside my car until he makes it into the house. It's nerve-racking, worrying that he'll fall.

The Men's Stag is held at the Lake Arrowhead Presbyterian Church in an annex room normally used for Sunday school.

On the walls are colorful maps of different countries around the globe, a chart of the alphabet, a portrait of Jesus. In one corner is a baby's playpen full of all kinds of toys. Volunteers from our group arrive early to put out tables for A.A. literature, get the coffee brewing, and set up the steel foldout chairs. My friend Dave buys a cushy armchair for Nick at a garage sale, it's stored in the closet here, and the volunteers put it out, too. At first I worried that Nick would be offended by this small kindness, but thankfully I'm wrong, and this is a good thing. Pride is no reason for the terminally ill to deny themselves the simple comfort of a soft chair.

The men here come from all walks of life. We are doctors and lawyers. We are construction workers and short-order cooks. Produce clerks and salesmen and teachers. Some of us are out of work, having been fired or let go, or we're unemployable because we can't stay sober long enough to keep a job. This meeting is popular on the mountain, regularly attracting fifty men or more, and I don't think a single one of us over the age of forty hasn't been married and divorced at least once. We talk about broken families. We talk about bankruptcy and homes lost to foreclosure. We talk about child support and custody battles and blame the courts in California for always siding with the woman and driving us to do things we later come to regret. The things men say when women are not around are often bitter and crude, and I sometimes wonder if the women-only meeting is anything like ours. I imagine it is. Nick can hold his own against the most angry and foulmouthed among us, just as I can if I choose, but instead he likes to steer the conversation in a different direction. He likes to talk about *staying in the solution* and *the gifts of sobriety* and getting back what we lost to alcoholism, our morals and ethics, our sense of truth and fairness. He likes to talk about gratitude and how alcoholism and drug addiction are only symptoms of the graver, underlying problems of selfishness and ego.

He demands our respect because his words are heartfelt and make us think about our lives and sobriety in ways we otherwise might not. Now, because he is not long for the world, the men seem to listen more closely than ever, expecting to hear the sort of wisdom only a dying man can offer, but there is nothing profound about death, no great enlightenment as a result of its approach, and if there is something to learn in Nick's passing, it is, for me, the grace with which he comes to accept it.

In my mind I can still hear Nick.

I can still hear his reassuring words of strength and hope reverberating through the years as he listened to me when we did my Fourth and Fifth Steps together, the ones designed to clear the conscience of the things that lead people like us to seek refuge in alcohol and drugs. Nick knew more about me than any person on earth, and I am certain that he has done as he had promised, taking my darkest secrets to his grave.

The day arrives when I call before I leave the university to pick him up for the Men's Stag, and his wife answers, telling me that he's sleeping.

"I don't want to wake him," she says. "He's been really tired these last couple days. Why don't you guys shoot for next week? I'm sure he'll feel better by then."

But it's the same story when next week rolls around.

From what I understand, Nick makes the decision himself. His wife and children protest, they want to take care of him to the very end, but he won't have it. I suspect they see it as their duty.

I suspect they see it as a testament to their love and loyalty, and I imagine that they assure him, over and over, that even bedridden he is no burden. I admire them for this. It is the right and noble thing for them to want to do, but it is also the right and noble thing for Nick to decide otherwise. Because he *will* be a burden. Because his needs *will* intensify. The proper place to die may or may not be in the foreign environment of hospice care at our local mountain hospital but it is the choice my friend makes. I do not count the days between the time he checks into hospice and the time that our visits end. It could have been a couple of weeks. I don't believe it stretched beyond three.

The first time I visit, it's with about a dozen others from A.A. Ordinarily the hospital doesn't allow more than two or three visitors at a time, but someone in our group makes special arrangements with whoever is in charge of these things and we hold a kind of mini-meeting for Nick. He has a good room. It is a private room with a window offering a peek of the lake, but it is also very small. We can't all fit inside. There is hardly space enough for a single bed, a chair, an end table, and an IV stand, so a few of us have to remain in the hallway, just outside the door. Those closest to Nick are huddled around his bed, some standing, some sitting on the edge of the mattress. There is a row behind them, and then another, which includes me. He is only a few feet away but I can hardly see him for the people in front of me. Occasionally, when someone shifts their weight, or turns to one side or the other, I glimpse him in the bed, a skeleton of a man in a hospital gown with an IV in his arm, the needle secured with a strip of surgical tape.

Someone is talking.

"You remember the time . . ."

The words trail off. I'm not listening. My mind drifts and I find myself looking out the window at what little I can see of the lake, a sliver of it, far in the distance, the sun's rays refracting and bending along the smooth surface of the water. I hear another voice. "And how about that time when . . ." But again my mind strays. Again I find myself not listening. Although I am a member of this group, and although I respect everyone for coming to see Nick today, I somehow feel as if I don't belong, that I'm some kind of stranger, and that my friend, like the lake I'm staring at, is somewhere else, somewhere far away. I know it is good that we are all here. I know it is good for Nick to see that so many care about him, as I know he cares about them, and yet, strangely, I feel that our coming here as a group is somehow invasive, somehow undignified. One guy is crying, quietly, while another is laughing at something Nick has said. Those who can't fit into the room, the ones standing in the hallway outside the door, I doubt they can hear much of what Nick or the others are saying. If I want his attention, I'll have to compete for it. I'll have to raise my voice. I'll have to shoulder my way through the crowd, get closer to the bed, and I don't want to do that.

So after a while I decide to slip out. I try to catch Nick's eye as I leave, so I can give a quick wave goodbye, but he is busy talking to someone else and doesn't see me. I tell myself that I'll visit again when it's just the two of us. That's how it should be. That's how I need it to be, and the next day I call the front desk to find out when it's okay for me to drop by.

"Are you family?"

"No," I say. "But we're good friends."

"The family requests his privacy now," she says. "I'm sure you understand."

She's about to hang up. I can sense it, and so I'm fast. There's urgency in my voice.

"Can I at least talk to him? Can you put me through to his room?"

"What's your name?"

"Jim Brown," I say.

"Hang on," she says.

She puts me on hold. Maybe a minute passes, I don't know, but it feels longer. Eventually she gets back to me.

"Here he is," she says.

There's a clicking noise, one line disconnecting, another opening. Then there's Nick's voice.

"How you doing?"

"Good," I say.

"Can you bring me a pizza?"

"What?"

"Pizza," he says. "Can you bring me a pizza?"

I'm caught off guard. I'm a little slow to respond.

"I would if I could," I say, "but they said only family is allowed to visit."

"I'll take care of that," he says, "you take care of the pizza. Make sure you get it from The Cottage. With extra anchovies. New York style," he says. "None of that Domino's shit. When can you come by?"

"Right now if you want."

"That's perfect."

I worry that they won't let me bring in a pizza. For all I know they don't want him eating something like this, that maybe his doctors think it's too greasy or rich, that it'll make him sick, but I buy him one anyway. I get it from The Cottage, too, a local Italian restaurant known on the mountain for the best pizza. I get a small one, and so far as worrying about bringing it in, the two women at the nurse's station don't blink an eye. They just ask for my name and have me sign the visitor's sheet, give me his room number, which I already know, and then point me in the right direction. As I make my way down the hall, the smell of Pine-Sol masking the odors of sickness triggers memories of others I've loved and lost in hospitals, and I have to make a conscious effort to push those thoughts, images, and feelings aside. I am here to see my friend. I need to be in good spirits, but it can't be faked or forced. This is also not the time to be sullen. I know he wouldn't want that, either.

I stand in the doorway.

"What took you so long? Come on in," he says. "Shut the door."

Nick is sitting upright in bed. He smiles. I smile back and set the box of pizza on his lap. Immediately he flips open the top and grabs a piece with his free hand. The other, or his arm, anyway, it's hooked up to an IV with a tube running from the bag to a needle in the crook of his elbow. There's a speck of blood showing through the surgical tape where the needle meets the vein.

He holds the box out to me.

"Want a piece?"

I shake my head.

"Not with anchovies."

"Suit yourself," he says. "More for me."

He waves a slice under his nose. Sniffs. Closes his eyes. Takes a bite.

"Ah," he says, as he chews, "you have no idea how wonderful this tastes after all those months on that crazy diet. Fine good it did, huh? Hey," he says, "check it out." He passes his finger over a little red button on the bed railing. "When I press this, the nurse comes running. Know what I get? Morphine. A sweet spike of nirvana." Heroin had been his drug of choice, and though morphine isn't quite on the same level, it's close. "Of course they get all pushed out of shape when they think I'm hitting the button too much. Amateurs," he says, "they couldn't dose an old junkie right if their lives depended on it. We have a built-in tolerance. I've tried to educate them but they don't seem to get it." He winks at me. "I'm working on the doc to switch me over to Dilaudid."

Dilaudid is better than morphine, but so far this stuff seems to be doing the job. Nick is high. And I'm glad for him. Relieved of the intense pain, or much of it I hope, it's as if he's making something of a comeback. He's more vibrant. He looks healthier. Even his cheeks have some color in them again. At this rate, with a little luck and more fatty foods, he might last longer than the doctors think. I heard through the grapevine that they're not giving him more than a week.

"Next time you come," he says, "bring me some Ben and Jerry's."

"What kind?"

"Cookie dough. A quart."

"A quart? You can't eat a quart."

"Oh yeah," he says, "watch me."

There's one chair in the room. I scoot it close to his bed and sit down beside him.

Nick finishes his piece of pizza and starts on another, but he sets it down after the first bite. I can tell he's getting ahead of himself and needs to take it slower. Morphine and food don't go well together. He presses a different button on the railing of the bed and the back of it rises, so he's sitting more upright than before.

For a while we're quiet. He's high. He has what they call *heroin eyes*. Whereas the pupils dilate on coke or meth, they shrink on opiates, and Nick's are pinheads. He's starting to drift. "She was a cute little thing. Sugar Brown," he says. "This was back in the day," he says, "when getting high was still good. Because it wasn't always bad, you know, or I never would've started. I was in my twenties. She was nineteen." He reaches for the plastic cup of water on the end table, but it's a strain, so I get it for him. His lips are dry. He takes a sip and continues. "She was a stripper. She did bachelor parties and it was my job to keep the animals from going crazy. Didn't I already tell you this story?" I tell him no, and it's true. There's so much I don't know about him, and I like that he's drifting back, returning to better times. I tell him to keep going. This is good for him. This is good for me. "Sometimes there was trouble. Sometimes some fool would grab her ass and I'd have to step up, but usually things went smooth. She put on a hell of a show. Sugar was hot." He pauses, as if he's picturing her. "That girl made some big bucks. She might do three or four gigs a night, and after she was done we'd drive to the connect's house. This is Boston. It would be three or four o'clock in the morning and we'd score a few balloons and drive back to her place. She had this little apartment in Roxbury near the T. I can still see her, Jimmy, jumping up and down on the bed on her cute little bare feet, screaming '*me first, me first.*' I'm trying to cook it up and keep from laughing and you know how it is, how you have to have a steady hand." Nick laughs, and it strikes me, as I laugh with him, how I haven't heard this kind of laugh from him, a good deep laugh, since he was given the bad news. I don't have the timeline straight but I know it's been well over two years. The part about the steady hand, that has to do with balancing a spoon filled with water and heroin while you hold the flame from a lighter underneath it.

The morphine high has peaks and valleys and his eyes are growing heavy. For a while he's quiet again. I'm wondering if he knows that I'm still here when he slowly looks over at me and blinks.

"Where was I?"

"I think you're getting sleepy," I say.

"Maybe a little," he says, "but you don't have to go."

"I probably should. You need your rest."

"You're coming back, though."

"Sure," I say. "I'll bring some Ben and Jerry's."

His eyes shut. The best I can figure is that the nurse dosed him just before I came, and he's hit the peak, what junkies call *the nod*. He's somewhere else now. I hope so, anyway. I want him to dream. I want him to drift back to a better place where there is no pain or sickness and he is healthy and young again and getting high is still good. I want it to seem that way for him even though I know it is and can never be anything other than a lie. The initial rush, maybe it's wonderful, but the coming down part and having to fix again and again to keep the depression at bay, that always ends up being about desperation and misery, especially when there is nothing left to fix and the panic sets in. The good thing about his situation here is that he doesn't have to worry about running out of drugs.

I don't go back for several days. Visiting hours are over by the time I get off work. But when the weekend rolls around, on a Saturday afternoon, I stop at the supermarket, buy a quart of Ben and Jerry's cookie dough ice cream, and then head over to the hospital. In this short span of less than a week, despite the morphine and pizza and whatever other fatty foods his wife and kids have probably brought him, he's lost more weight. The bones in his face are sharply defined and his neck seems too thin for the size and heaviness of his skull. His eyes, they're sunken and drawn, and the color that had briefly returned to his cheeks just a few days ago is gone again. His skin is ashen. His lips are dry and tight as if they're stiffening into his gums, and when he smiles, because he manages a smile when I come through the door, it looks like it hurts him.

I have the ice cream in a white bag. I pull it out and show him.

"Just what the doctor ordered," I say.

"Cookie dough?"

"Cookie dough," I say.

"You bring a spoon?"

"Absolutely."

They had some plastic ones at the pastry counter inside the grocery store, and I grabbed a couple of them on my way out. I dig into my back pocket where I stashed the spoons. He presses the button on his bed so that he's sitting upright.

I take the top off the ice cream. I set the carton in his lap along with one of the spoons.

"Okay," I say. "Dig in. You wanted a full quart, you got it. Now you have to eat the whole thing. I'm not leaving until you do."

He wants to laugh, and he does, or he tries to anyway, but it's strained and weak and turns into a cough. It's plain that Nick can't hold the carton and a spoon at the same time, and I realize what an idiot I am. How I shouldn't have given it to him without a second thought. How I shouldn't have come in acting cavalier and trying to be funny. It was stupid of me and I regret placing him in the position of my having to take the ice cream away and set it on the end table.

Somebody else, probably his wife or one of his daughters, must've recently visited because the one chair in the room is already situated close to his bed. I sit in it. His frail hands are folded neatly in his lap and I want to reach for them. I want to take his hand in mine but I don't. I'm not sure if it's the right thing to do. If he would want that. I have never held his hand before and I worry that if I hold it now he may feel that I am in some way affirming his passing. Maybe the affirmation of touch is the sole domain of his wife and children. So I'm surprised then when he places his hand on top of mine.

"It's all good," he says. "The attic is clear."

That's an inside thing, about the attic.

For Nick and me, it means the conscience, and how, as

alcoholic-addicts, we have to crawl way back inside our heads. Knock off the cobwebs. Sort through the junk. Figure out what's worth keeping and what's not. It can be a great ride down memory lane or a painful one that leads us to dark places we'd rather not revisit. The idea, in the end, is to value the moment and live in it, the here and now.

"You have to get rid of all your old skeletons," he told me, when we were working together on keeping me sober. "Bone by bone. Smash them to pieces. Crush them to dust. No more beating yourself up about *why did this happen* or *what if I'd done that.* You toss out the garbage of the past so you can make room for all the good in the present. You want to get a running start on a whole new life."

There are a lot of skeletons up in my head, as there are in Nick's, but so long as we clear them out every now and then, we'll be okay. And it's not like one cleaning does the trick. Some skeletons get overlooked. New ones somehow work their way in between the cracks. The bones need to be broken up, bagged, and thrown out on a regular basis, learning from the process, then letting go and moving on.

One of his daughters comes into the room. She has Nick's light blue eyes. She's a good, hardworking young woman putting herself through college. I get to my feet.

"You don't have to go," Nick says.

But I know I do. I know he's just being polite.

"She outranks me," I say, and by this I mean that it's best he spend this time alone with his daughter.

I know my place, and I know, too, as I walk out of the room

that day that I won't see him again. He'll make it through the night but not the next.

My car is parked in the section reserved for visitors. I unlock the door. I slip behind the wheel. But instead of starting the engine and driving off, I just sit there, looking out the window. A woman in hospital scrubs pushes a little girl in a wheelchair past the gardenia bushes in the flowerbeds out front. She looks over her shoulder at the woman, then points to something on the ground, and I think about Nick. I think about the man I never met, shivering and shaking in the alleyways of the old Bowery in New York, looking for his next fix. By then no one would have wanted anything to do with him. Not family. Not friends. He is at once already dead, and when my time comes I want my boys and wife to say I died twice, too, only they don't recall much about that other man. The alcoholic. The addict. The one they remember most is a good and sober father and husband. He learns to love, maybe for the first time, and in return they come to forgive and love him.

My cell rings. I answer it.

"Where are you?" Nate says.

"I'm on my way," I say.

"You were supposed to be here an hour ago. I wrestle for first place in twenty minutes."

Nate is the last of my wrestlers. My two other boys have grown up and moved out, and I can't miss this match. There won't be many more to watch. I tell him I'll be there soon and hang up. Fortunately the tournament is at the local high school, an easy ten minutes from the hospital, so I'll make it.

As I start the engine, I notice the woman in scrubs picks something up off the ground and puts it in the little girl's hand. It's just a shiny rock, a pebble really, but it's how she stares at it, her mouth agape, that gives me pause. She is in absolute awe, and for a moment, looking at her, so am I.

Stories

My friend Dave calls every now and then and asks me to go to a meeting with him. My friend Dave says that if he goes more than a few days without a meeting that he feels restless, irritable, and discontented. This is exactly what the Big Book of A.A. tells us about alcoholics—that we are, by nature, a colicky bunch who need to be continually reminded that life isn't as bad as we make it out to be. The sky is not falling every minute of the day. The world isn't out to get us. And not everyone in it is an asshole, though I sometimes feel certain of this, particularly when I'm driving.

"Miss a few meetings," Dave tells me, "and I'm right back to my own stinking thinking and that much closer to the next drink." He wags his head. "I don't know how you do it, man. I just know I can't."

He's referring to my falling away from A.A. Where in the first few years of my sobriety, I went to meetings regularly, usually four or five a week, when I get up to around eight years sober, I find myself going to one or two a week. Then it's one every other week. Then once a month. During the entire ninth year of my sobriety, I think I attend a total of six or seven meetings. I even skip taking my ten-year chip, which, when you reach the double-digit mark of sobriety, is considered a pretty big deal.

Which it is.

That's a long time to be sober for someone who's more or less spent the previous four decades of his time on this planet under the influence of booze or some other drug. And it's not that I'm not grateful. It's not that being clean and sober hasn't made a tremendous difference in the quality and purpose of my life. It has. It's just that I don't feel the same *pull*, the same *need* to attend meetings as I once did, because I'm more secure about not drinking and using. I don't think about it but rarely, and even then the thought is fleeting. Frankly the idea of getting drunk or high again repulses me, which by no means implies that I think I'm impervious to drinking again. Only a fool, or an alcoholic, would buy that. As for the Big Book itself, where I used to crack it open when I went to bed—any chapter or page would do—or read from it a few minutes when I woke up in the morning, for the last couple of years it's been gathering dust on the bookshelf in my bedroom. I used to read it at night as a kind of salutation for making it another twenty-four hours without a drink. I used to read it in the morning to help prepare me for the chaos of the day ahead. I used to meditate, too, as the Big Book recommends, to improve my conscious contact with God. And pray, I used to pray several times a day, and now I'm lucky if I don't forget to do it once before I turn out the lights for the night. It's not as if I haven't already read it cover to cover a couple times, not counting all the book study meetings I've attended, where as a group I've gone over it page by page, line by line. I tell myself I'm too busy to sponsor anyone now. I don't remember the last time I visited a prison to tell the cons there's a better way to live.

Another reason I've fallen away, and it's not something I like to talk about, has to do with Nick's death. He was like my buddy Dave in that he really enjoyed meetings and didn't want to miss many, because, at least in part, he liked the social aspect of A.A. He had all kinds of friends there. He was respected. When he shared, people listened, because he always had something valuable to say. More importantly, he believed in being there for the newcomers. To set an example. To give hope to those struggling to get their first thirty days, or first day, period. He said he never forgot his darkest days of suffering, and he used them to remind himself that one of the main purposes of his life, along with being a good father and husband, was to help others avoid the suffering he went through. I remember him telling a guy in his twenties that if he could get clean and sober now, while he was still a young man, he could save himself a lifetime of pain and grief.

Nick lasted a year longer than the two his doctors predicted after they diagnosed him. By then I was closing in on six years of sobriety. He's been gone about five years now, and I still miss those days when I used to pick him up and take him to the Men's Stag. I valued our time together all the more because I knew it was running out and I didn't want it to end. But of course it did, and when he died, something in me died, too, as it did when I lost others I loved. Nick was a friend, sure, but he was also my mentor and sponsor who cared about me when I didn't care about myself. He gave me hope when I had none. I'd be lying if I said I didn't seriously consider getting drunk and high again in the days after he'd passed, and since then every meeting I've attended makes me think of him. Not that this is a bad thing. It isn't. If Nick could talk to me, I know he'd tell me exactly what Dave does.

The relapse starts when you stop meetings.

You don't *not* go to meetings because they remind you of those you've lost any more than you wouldn't honor Memorial Day if you had a close friend or loved one who paid the ultimate price for this country.

"If anything," Dave says, "that's *more reason* to go."

I know he's right, but like a typical alcoholic, I immediately go into judgment mode. In my head I make a list of all the things I don't like about A.A. Some of the people in those rooms are real jerks. I don't want to see them. I don't want to hear them. Some of the old-timers have thirty years or more of sobriety and I don't believe for a second that they're at risk of getting drunk again. They come to A.A. now because they're retired and lonely and bored. Others aren't real alcoholics or addicts but like being part of the group. Some are only there to get their court cards signed because they got a DUI and the judge ordered them to attend a bunch of meetings as a condition of their probation. Some are mentally tweaked and it has nothing to do with drugs or alcohol. Some are drifters taking advantage of the free donuts, cookies, and coffee. Still others are little more than problem teenagers whose parents catch them with drugs and send them to rehab, and then rehab, as part of their recovery program, sends them to A.A.

How about the Big Book itself, its outdated language and figures of speech? The younger, less forgiving generations consider much of it laughable. That chapter "To Wives" would get the author Bill Wilson in some real trouble today.

As for the anonymity part and all that stuff about *what you hear here, let it stay here,* it's a joke. At the start of each meeting, to be honest, the leader should announce that whatever you share with the group can and will be used for the amusement and pleasure of the gossips in the room. And that includes about everyone. *Principles before personalities* is another of A.A.'s favorite sayings, and it's a fine ideal to aspire to, but many of us nonetheless harbor deep resentments toward each other. There's also the issue of A.A. being a cult with the sole purpose of converting and brainwashing you into becoming one of its mindless clones. Then you have your obnoxious A.A. gurus who love to enlighten those who might question their infinite wisdom by pontificating about their superior sense of spirituality and humility.

As with any gathering of humans, there is conflict, tension, the clash of ideas and opinions, and yet, despite all the critical things I could point out about A.A., like a typical alcoholic, I overlook the good. In the newcomer, I see myself, and in seeing myself, I recall my early struggles. Like Nick, maybe I ought not to forget them. Maybe these memories are tools. In the old-timers, instead of dismissing them as bored and lonely, I could see them as successful examples of long-term sobriety. What right, by the way, do I have to say what they should or shouldn't do with their days? For those who annoy me for their bluster and ego, why can't I tune them out and focus on those whose stories are genuine and true? What of the repentant? What lesson is there in someone coming to terms with the pain and sorrow their drinking has caused others and who now want nothing more than to repair what they fear may be irreparable? That person talking might as well be me, and the lesson I can't forget is recognizing that by no means or measure am I unique.

Without A.A., this story wouldn't be written.

Without A.A., I wouldn't have met Nick, either, and he's a chapter in my recovery that I celebrate every day that I don't take a drink.

So, the next time my friend Dave calls and asks me to go to a meeting, I can say, no, I'm busy. Maybe some other time. I'm doing fine on my own.

Or, the next time he calls, I can say yes.

Better still, I'll show up at a meeting and surprise him.

It's time to dust off that Big Book. It's time to remember Nick and how he never let himself forget the darkest days as well as the few good ones, way back in the beginning, when getting wasted still seemed fun. It's time to sit up straight and pay attention again.

I need to listen to the stories.

I need to see myself in them. I need to tell my own story and believe, in telling it, that someone might see themselves in me. In embracing the lives of other drunks, I embrace the tattered remains of my own past, and it's together, not alone, that we tell our stories with the hope of saving a life, one that belongs to us all.

Acknowledgments

For this book I'm indebted to my editor Dan Smetanka and my agent Ryan Harbage. For the love of my sons, Andy, Logan, and Nate, I am blessed and grateful. For their friendship and support, I thank Dave Dohoda, Chet Hower, Tim M., Orlando Ramirez, and Vicky Stebbings, as I do Lesley and Greg Firmin who continue to celebrate the lives of my brother and sister. And, as always, I thank my wonderful wife, Paula Priamos-Brown, for helping me to write this book.

© Nate Brown

JAMES BROWN is the author of the critically acclaimed memoirs *The Los Angeles Diaries* and *This River*. He is the recipient of a National Endowment for the Arts Literature Fellowship and the Nelson Algren Literary Award in short fiction. Brown's work has appeared in *GQ*, *The New York Times Magazine*, *Los Angeles Times Magazine*, *Ploughshares*, *New England Review*, and many other publications. He lives in Lake Arrowhead, California.